God's Plan for Heaven, Eternity and the Universe Explained

Despite knowing humans would sin, learn why God creating the human race was the GREATEST thing He has ever done and probably will do in all eternity!

Written by
David M. Cogburn

Contents

Synopsis

I would like to begin by thanking my wonderful wife, Pamela, for continually encouraging me to write this book. The title of this book - God's Plan for Heaven, Eternity and the Universe is "exactly" that. This book will help you to easily understand God's plan from the beginning of creation all the way to when the human race is over and everyone is living inside eternity with God or separated from God. The ONLY thing that matters for every human being is ETERNITY and ALL of God's plan is about how to know Him and spend it with Him. This book is very "different". It is written for "everyone" from people with little or no Bible knowledge to even people with advanced knowledge of the Bible who will learn things that most have never even thought about before.

God creating human beings knowing we would sin against Him from the very beginning and be born with a sin nature is by far the **GREATEST thing** God has **ever done and will probably be the greatest thing He will ever do in all of eternity.** The pleasure we bring Him is incalculable, as you will see. This book will help you to understand not only WHAT God has done in His plan but more **IMPORTANTLY WHY** He has done it the way He has done it. Many will think this book is simply my opinion, but everything in this book is based "**directly**" on God's Word in the Bible or "**indirectly**" based on what God has done according to His **direct** Word in the Bible.

Many of you know or suspect we are living in the end times just before the rapture followed by Jesus' 2nd coming, which is, obviously, a **MAJOR** part of God's plan. There are a lot of details in this book to explain the end times and why it is **our generation** that should experience Jesus' 2nd coming and how truly close we are to it.

This book will help you to understand God's plan and the Bible in a way most of you have never known before and will surprise you in a most pleasurable way. Also, hopefully, this book will help draw many of you to God or back to God depending on your current relationship with Him. My main prayer is that everyone on the planet could read this book in order to spend eternity with God but, obviously, all of that is in God's hands. I truly believe most of you will enjoy this book by discovering many things you are currently not aware of. May God bless each and every one of you who ventures into God's Plan for Heaven, Eternity and the Universe Explained.

God's Plan for Heaven, Eternity and the Universe Explained

Let's start off with a rhetorical question. Which is more important – life on earth or life in eternity?

The most dangerous thing to every human being on the planet now and for always is "free will" because with it we determine our eternal destiny. We are all "eternal" spiritual beings temporarily residing in a human body until we enter eternity at death. And the most important thing about eternity is where we spend it - either with God forever or separated from God forever.

Like real estate, eternity is all about location, location, location. What is a 100-year human life span compared to 1000 trillion years times 1000 trillion years and you are just beginning? Nothing but nothing but nothing matters more than eternity and where you spend it. May this book help you find the truth of the right location.

PURPOSE FOR EVERYTHING

Some of the most important questions we can ask ourselves is why are we here? What is the purpose of life? Why did God create us in the first place?

The obvious answer is for His pleasure or because He wanted to but is there more to it than that? There is a "lot" more to it than that and the answer will shock you as you will see. The answer to this question can only come from His word in the Bible and what it says about everything He's already done in the past and everything He's going to do in the future. And I will "prove" to you later how the Bible and the Bible "alone" truly is the "verifiable" word of God. So, let's jump in and see what we can figure out.

KNOWLEDGE OF GOD AND HIS PLAN

The vast majority of people on earth know very little to nothing about God and certainly not about His plan for mankind. There are many people who call themselves atheists, agonistics or unbelievers in God. There are also many people who do believe in God but know very little beyond that in terms of how to truly know Him and even fewer people who believe in God and who actually "do" know Him through a personal intimate relationship with Him. Which category do you fall into?

Even if you have never read one word of the Bible, which is called the Word of God, by the time you finish this book your understanding of

God, God's plan in the Bible and what He's up to will be off the charts compared to where you are now.

This also applies to people who have read the Bible but have trouble understanding it. There are even people who are experts of the Bible who I'm pretty sure will learn things in this book they never thought about before.

I will provide an "easy understanding" of God's plan from the very beginning of everything, including the human race, to the very end when there are no more humans and show who belongs to God and will live with Him forever.

To keep this book reasonably short I will focus mainly on the "highlights" of God's plan throughout the Bible. However, since we are living in the end times I will go into more detail about what is still yet to come and how God wraps things up. I have just made a very "bold" statement. Let's see what evidence there is for that statement.

HOW IT BEGAN

In the beginning was God. Here is the simplest fact there is: It is "impossible" for "something" to come from "nothing," period. It takes "something" to create something. Only God is different because God did not come from "something." He is "THE SOMETHING" that has always existed no matter how impossible it is for us to understand that, and He is "THE SOMETHING" that has created "everything!"

THE UNIVERSE

Everything that is "visible" was "created by a creator," whether it is the universe or a chair. The biggest "visible something" that was created that we can see is, obviously, the universe. For those who like to think the universe somehow created itself, ask yourself this question: How could a universe that somehow created itself out of chaos create humans who can THINK, REASON, HAVE EMOTIONS, CREATE, and HAVE A PAST, PRESENT AND FUTURE? You should win the Pulitzer Prize if you figure that one out.

SUPERNATURAL VS NATURAL

We are human beings who live in that "universe." It is no surprise that Whoever created us and the universe is far, far greater than we are or can even imagine. We refer to that Person as Creator God. He is Supernatural and we are natural. We normally think of the Supernatural as something that is beyond human capability and what we consider "impossible" such as creating a planet might be difficult for us; don't you think?

Supernatural vs natural is a HUGE problem and stumbling block for many people and as a result causes them to not believe in God or His Bible. What is the definition of Supernatural? It means God did it, period. There is "nothing natural" about God - only SUPERnatural.

Why is the Supernatural a problem for many? They reject it for one main reason. They compare God to us and bring God down to OUR level.

When they see some of the miracles in the Bible such as parting of the Red Sea, raising the dead, having a donkey speak, Jesus turning water into wine, Jesus calming a raging sea, feeding 5000 with a loaf of bread and a couple of fish or His resurrection and many other miracles, they say, "That's impossible! No one can do any of those things." And they are right - no "human" can do any of those things. But for a Creator God who showed His infinite power by creating everything, is there "anything" too difficult for Him? I hope that is a rhetorical question.

Our way of thinking and understanding is vastly different when we compare man to God's level. In Numbers 22 in the Bible it says that a donkey "spoke" to Balaam. If I read in the Bible that a "chair" started speaking to the people, my first reaction would "not" be that's impossible. It would be now, that's interesting. I wonder why God did it that way? When you "recognize" who God truly is, and look at us from His level, you have zero problems with "anything" Supernatural in the Bible.

VISIBLE INVISIBILITY

A major problem for much of mankind is that Creator God is "invisible" to us now. So how can we know He exists and especially how can we have any kind of relationship with someone who is invisible?

Since He created us, He knew He needed to communicate to us in a way we could understand. His "invisibility" becomes "visible" to all of us in two major ways - through His creation and through His Word in the Bible which is called the Word of God.

The universe and all creation reveal to us there "is" a God. His Word in the Bible reveals His plan for how everything begins and ends and instructions to mankind on how to not only know Him but also how we are to live our lives in terms of relationships, how we are to treat one another, finances, governments and literally every aspect of life on earth.

When Creator God tells us how to do "anything," it should not be difficult to understand how His way is always the "best" way compared to mankind's way. Some say the word "Bible" is an acronym that stands for:

Basic Instructions Before Leaving Earth which turns out that is exactly what it is. As I just said a moment ago, later in this book I will show you how we can "easily" know that the Bible truly is the Supernatural word of God compared to any other books that have ever been written.

WHICH RELIGIONS ARE CORRECT?

There are many different religions that tell us how to get to God. Is it possible that all of them are correct or only a few are correct or is it possible that only one is correct? In this book I will address "why" we believe what we believe and how we can know which so-called religion is correct when it comes to knowing God.

GOD'S ATTRIBUTES

The Bible tells us that God is a "Triune" God who is comprised of three different Essences: Father, Son and Holy Spirit. He is one God with three Essences. A good earthly example is water. Water can be a solid, liquid or gas but is still water. Think of the Father as the Solid, the Son as the Liquid and the Holy Spirit as the Gas.

So, what is the number one attribute of God? Is it omniscience (all knowing), omnipotence (all powerful), omnibenevolence (Holy and supremely good) or is it Love? This may surprise you, but the number one attribute of God is none of those. His number one attribute is the "theme" of this book. Nothing matters to God more than His number one attribute. It is called "Relationship."

God Himself is a three-in-one Relationship and relationship is what brings God His greatest joy and pleasure. A Divine three-in-one Relationship is what God IS and has always been - long before He created anything.

God is, obviously, also all knowing, all powerful, Holy and supremely good and is a God of love as well as many other wonderful attributes.

Everything we have seen God do in all of His creation is about mainly one thing - relationships, as you will see.

ANGELS AND RELATIONSHIP

God loves relationships so much He decided to create more of it by creating angels to have a personal relationship with Himself and with each other. He created each angel to be like Himself in terms of holy, perfect and without sin. That is God's "STANDARD" and every sentient being that God creates He creates that way. His angels live in His presence in heaven and enjoy the very best He has to offer.

We all know or should know God is also a God of love. Love is simply putting others before yourself. Pride is putting yourself before others. You cannot have love unless you have the ability not to love. This is called free will. Without free will God's created beings would simply be robots and it is impossible to have a "true relationship" with a robot for obvious reasons.

Robots will never have free will or think or feel or have emotions for themselves. No matter how sophisticated they are now or become in the future, all they will ever be able to do is "compute" what they are programmed to do. Robots are the closest thing that man can create that resembles human beings.

True "life" is reserved for God alone. A good example is blood. The Bible says there is life in the blood and God is the creator of life - all life. With all of our technology, there still is no substitute for blood.

God loves His angels, and they love Him back. Then the unthinkable happened. Lucifer, God's highest created angel, took his eyes off God and put them on himself when he decided he, too, wanted to be like God and be worshiped.

This is the first "sin" recorded in the Bible - the sin of pride when Lucifer put himself before God. This resulted in him rejecting the best God had to offer and his influence with the other angels caused one-third of God's angels to also fall when they, too, rejected the best God had to offer them.

God being all knowing, of course, knew long before He even created His angels this would occur. It still saddened Him though to see one-third of His created angels reject Him and it appears it may have been around this point in eternity that God may have had "this type of thought" based on what has happened since then: "I have created my holy sinless angels to live in My presence and enjoy the best I have to offer them and still one-third of them have rejected Me. Hmmm, what if I now create a different type of being - human beings?

They will be the opposite of my angels in every way. I will create a universe for them. I know they will sin from the very beginning and every human being will be born "lost" and spiritually dead with a sin nature and will not live in My presence and receive the best I have to offer and they will have to take care of themselves."

WHAT??? Why would God want to do something like that? This sounds crazy. The answer will "astound" you! Stay tuned.

ETERNITY

Again, God is eternal and lives in eternity. Eternity is something that cannot be measured. It is simply forever and has no end. All of God's holy attributes and goodness dwell in eternity and what happens in eternity "STAYS" in eternity. This is so important, let me type it again. What happens in eternity "STAYS" in eternity. This is "crucial" to God's plan.

There is no "annihilation" type of death in eternity - only a separation from God-type of death, which is far worse than annihilation. For example, the fallen angels have no plan of redemption - no way to ever get right with God again because what happens in eternity stays in eternity. And because of that, meaning no death, there is no one who could "die" in eternity to pay the price for their sins. Physical death can "only" occur inside God's universe He creates and there is a perfectly good reason for this as you are about to learn.

TIME

Since God now wants to create human beings who will begin life spiritually dead and born lost with a sin nature, He has to make sure NONE of this occurs "inside" eternity or we would all be "lost forever" "inside eternity" at birth.

Again, and I cannot emphasize this enough, what happens in eternity stays in eternity and this is why God decided to create a universe. One of the main purposes of the universe is to create time.

TIME exists "inside" eternity. Think of the universe and "time" as a "bubble" inside eternity. The problem for most of us is our visible bubble universe makes God's eternal world invisible to us now.

Only here can good and evil exist together and is the only place physical death can occur. Time and the universe have a beginning and an end and the Bible tells us when it all ends. More on that later.

Obviously, eternal God does not need time, but He knows that lost human beings will need "time" in order to come to know Him and have a personal intimate relationship with Him before entering into eternity when we die. This is why He created us in the first place - to have a personal intimate relationship with Him now and forever.

Here is a question for you. What is the greatest gift and greatest curse at the same time that God has given us? It is "time." Why? Time is the greatest curse because time destroys "everything." Nothing can survive time. The whole universe and everything in it is dying which certainly includes us. The Bible tells us the wages of sin is DEATH and the universe is certainly proof of that.

Do you think anything in heaven or eternity is dying? That would be impossible. However, in the universe death is just a matter of "time," no pun intended.

Time is also the greatest gift because only "time" allows us to be able to come to "know" God through a personal intimate relationship with Jesus and go from being spiritually dead forever to being spiritually alive forever. I will explain how that all happens in a moment.

GOD'S PLAN BEGINS FOR MANKIND

God tells us point blank in His Word in the Bible that His plan is to spend eternity on earth with us human beings. WAIT! Aren't we sinners? Why would God want to spend eternity on earth with us sinners? Let's now examine what He did to begin His plan with mankind to bring this about.

He begins by creating the universe and creates our planet earth in the universe on which He will create mankind and reside with us in His presence forever. That is the first part of His "plan" that involves us. It does finally happen, but there are a few "bumps in the road" for 7000 years before it occurs. More on the 7000 years later.

UNIVERSE CREATED FOR MANKIND

One of the most amazing things we've ever seen is the universe itself which shows us God's infinite "power." The universe seems almost infinite in size with billions of galaxies and billions of stars in each one and try to get your head around this: This whole universe was created for "US

ALONE."

WHAT? You're crazy! How do we know that? To many people that statement alone will seem like the dumbest thing they have ever heard and for good "human" reasoning. With billions and billions of stars and galaxies, to think "we" are the only ones here seems ludicrous - even laughable. We can know that it is only for us because first and foremost Creator God says so. He tells us in His Word, which we'll get into, that His plan is to spend "eternity" on "earth" with us alone and not with other beings from other planets.

Over the past several decades there has been a proliferation of UFO sightings and even though there has never been an "official visitation" by them, there have been enough sightings and evidence to show they seem real. The obvious human thinking is they have to be from other planets but a more reasonable explanation is they are from a different "dimension" vs a different planet. And the Bible shows us they have been here before. I will talk about this more in depth later in the book.

MANKIND BEGINS FOLLOWED BY SIN

God begins in Genesis 1:1 by saying "In the beginning God created the heavens and the earth." He creates earth with everything on it in terms of plants, animals, fish, birds - ALL life - and last but not least, mankind. He creates Adam from the dirt of the ground and then creates Eve from Adam's rib. Both are created by God "directly" and both are created perfect, holy and sinless which again is God's "standard."

God tells them His plan is to live on earth with them and He will take care of everything. God wants Adam and Eve to demonstrate their love for Him through "obedience".

He creates a beautiful garden of Eden for them where He provides everything, and Adam and Eve will reside in His presence. There is only one command from God. He places a tree in the middle of the garden called the tree of the knowledge of good and evil, and He tells them they can eat fruit of all the other trees but stay away from the knowledge of good and evil tree because on the day they eat its fruit they will surely die.

Did you notice how Lucifer and the fallen angels sinned using only their free will? There was no tree of the knowledge of good and evil in heaven to tempt them for one simple reason - there is NO evil in heaven.

Adam and Eve also used their free will to disobey God by eating the fruit of the knowledge of good and evil tree but they did so under the "deception" of Satan when his lies to Eve caused her to take a bite of the forbidden fruit.

Sin is still sin, but somehow it appears that mankind's sin under Satan's deception seems "mitigated" in some way compared to the fallen angels' sin with their free will alone. Man's sin is redeemable due to happening inside "time" and the angels' sin is not redeemable due to happening inside "eternity."

Another huge problem for mankind is God banishing Lucifer, now called Satan, and his fallen angels to earth where they are the arch enemy to God and the human race and will do everything they can to thwart God's plans and to destroy us.

The Bible points out that God allows this as it is part of God's plan and points out that there is invisible spiritual warfare going on behind the scenes around us between God and Satan to intervene in human affairs.

Being spiritual beings vs human beings, Satan and the fallen angels are invisible to humans "most of the time." However, the Bible tells us Satan somehow was able to transform into a serpent, and he spoke to Eve in the garden and told her she would not die if she ate the forbidden fruit and that she would be like God if she did eat from the tree of the knowledge of good and evil.

He deceived her and she did eat the forbidden fruit followed by Adam also eating it. They then knew they had done wrong by disobeying God and when He came looking for them they had put on a fig leaf to cover their nakedness. Each played the blame game. Eve said the serpent had deceived her, and Adam said Eve had caused him to eat the forbidden fruit.

God then had a conversation with Satan, the serpent, and told him in Genesis 3:15, which is the first and most important prophecy in the Bible,

"I will put enmity between you and the woman and between your offspring and hers. He will crush your head and you will strike his heel." (NIV version)

Other versions refer to offspring as "seed" where God will come between Satan's seed (man's seed) and woman's seed.

There are only two seeds needed to create a human being - the seed from the man and the seed from the woman. God has just referred to the seed of man as Satan's seed when He tells Satan I will come between YOUR seed and woman's seed.

This is where our sin nature comes from - man's seed. God created man from the ground and woman from man and thus, it is only MAN who is "responsible" for the "original" sin.

This means every person born from that point on will be born with a sin nature that comes from man's seed beginning with Adam.

The reason Mary had to be a virgin when she gave birth to Jesus is so Jesus would not have a human father and also be born with a sin nature from the human father's seed.

There is no question Mary was the most blessed of all women ever created to be the one to give birth to God Jesus. Some will disagree with this, but Mary herself "did have" a sin nature because her biological father was a human with a sin nature. To believe differently means you either do not believe what God has said or you don't want to believe it or you don't understand what He said.

Looking at this from our human perspective, it only seems natural Mary of all women would need to be without sin, but since ONLY MAN is responsible for the "original sin," this means Jesus could be born from a woman with a sin nature and still be born without a sin nature.

Mary was "conceived" by the Holy Spirit and thus, Jesus' biological Father is God the Holy Spirit. This means Jesus is fully human but has no sin nature and lives a perfect holy sinless life in order to fulfill His mission to save mankind from our sins by being a perfect, holy, sinless sacrifice to pay for the sins of mankind.

The "He" that will crush Satan's head is Jesus Himself when He is resurrected from the dead. And crushing Satan's head is a mortal wound whereas Satan will only strike Jesus' heel when Jesus is crucified and this is a nonmortal wound.

This first prophecy in the Bible immediately following Adam and Eve's disobedience by eating the forbidden fruit is pointing to how God will save us in the future from our sins.

The original sin of Adam did bring physical and spiritual death to every human being from that point to the end of human beings which I will talk about later. Adam brought physical and spiritual death to the human race and Jesus brought us spiritual eternal life when He paid the price for our sins on the cross. Physical is temporary and spiritual is eternal.

A moment ago I mentioned how the Bible says that life is in the blood. Many people ask the question, "Why are all humans born with a sin nature for something Adam did in the beginning? That's not fair!"

It is because of his blood. Since Adam's seed has now become Satan's seed, this means every human being is born with a sin nature, but our sin nature actually comes from Adam's blood line produced by his seed.

Every human being born from Adam is "part" of Adam's bloodline which brings sin with physical and spiritual death. We are cursed because of Adam's bloodline, but we are saved and redeemed through Jesus' SPIRITUAL blood line which brings eternal life due to no sin. The Bible talks a lot about how we are cleansed by the blood of Jesus. It is "all" about His blood which gives us eternal spiritual life as we will see.

PROCREATION POINTS TO SIN

But let me first point out something very interesting. Did you notice how God made humans to have the "ability" to procreate? Why is that? God has always "directly" made all of His sentient beings Himself. He made each angel Himself, Adam and Eve Himself and later Jesus Himself.

When God creates a sentient being, that being always meets God's "standard" of being holy, perfect and without sin as in the case of angels, Adam and Eve and Jesus.

But because of the original sin from Adam, all humans who are born are created "indirectly" by God but "directly" by humans through procreation. This is because it takes sinful human beings to create more sinful human beings. God does not Himself "directly" make any sinful sentient beings. Only humans can do that. This also proves that because God made humans to be "able" to procreate that He knew they would sin from the beginning and need to procreate to continue the human race.

FOLLOWING THE ORIGINAL SIN:

Did you notice something interesting here? Before Adam and Eve's sin of disobedience, God is living with them on earth. At this time, He is on earth vs heaven. However, following Adam and Eve's sin, God banished Adam and Eve from the garden of Eden, and He left them to go back to heaven.

From that point until today God is invisible to us sinful human beings. We are not receiving God's best now in terms of God taking care of all of "everything" for us. We now have to take care of ourselves.

However, this does not mean that God has "totally" left us. Far from it. He has only "physically" left us. Spiritually, God is always heavily involved in our world in the things that happen and the lives of people. He has a plan for everything and even tells us what it is in His holy Bible.

ONLY THE UNIVERSE HAS OPPOSITES

Because of sin, we now live in a world that is full of both good and evil. This brings up another interesting thing to think about. Everything with God in heaven is good, perfect, and pleasurable since He is there. The Bible shows us God is LIGHT, and without Him there is darkness.

Because God banishes Satan and his fallen angels from heaven and His presence, He has to create a "place" where He is "not" present, and this is why He creates hell.

Hell is simply the opposite of heaven, God, and light. Because God does not dwell in hell, the total opposite of God is what you get there. Instead of everything being good, pleasurable and light, you have everything bad, torment vs pleasure and darkness vs light.

WHY DOES GOD'S PLAN ALLOW SPIRITUAL WARFARE?

Why do you think God did not immediately send Satan and his demons to hell but allows them as part of His plan to coexist invisibly alongside us humans in order to deceive us and keep us from knowing God?

This is speculation but does make sense. God is looking for humans who will fall in love with Him "despite" having a sin nature and "despite" being "tempted" by Satan as Eve was tempted by Satan in the Garden of Eden.

Satan's temptation to us comes from spiritual warfare, and invisibly behind the scenes we have God's angels battling against Satan's demons, not to save our physical lives, but only our spiritual lives. God shows us how to win this sin battle and He is looking for those who believe Him.

Back to heaven vs hell. Let's think of heaven and hell as colors. Heaven is white. White light is the combination of "all" colors. Hell is black and black is the absence of "all" colors. Eternity is two opposites - everything good for eternity with God vs everything bad for eternity without God.

What about the universe? It is not white or black. It is "gray" which is a combination of white and black. ONLY inside the universe with "time" does God "allow" good and evil to dwell "together".

Earth is full of opposites. We have good and evil, pleasure and pain, happiness and sadness and many, many more. We have day and night. Day is an example of light and life when we wake up and get busy doing life each day in the light. Night is an example of darkness and death when we "sleep" at night in the darkness.

WHY OPPOSITES?

Why do you think God did it this way? God does not tolerate sin when it comes to salvation. He judges it, but He allows it during our human existence in the universe.

I think it is mainly because there are only two "eternal" opposites on earth - coming to know and embrace God for all eternity or rejecting God for all eternity. Everything is "about" eternity. Nothing truly matters but eternity and it all revolves around God.

Since everything with God is goodness, pleasure, joy, happiness, etc., He wants us to experience a "tiny preview" of what anything "good" is like on earth and I use the word "tiny" to show that "good" in humanity cannot begin to compare to the much greater "good" inside eternity with God.

And the opposite is true for everything bad on earth - evil, pain, sadness, etc. He wants us to experience a "tiny preview" of what anything "bad" is like on earth. I again use the word "tiny" to show the bad in humanity cannot begin to compare to the much greater "bad" inside eternity in hell without God.

I made up a bumper sticker slogan a few years ago that sort of describes it this way: Earth is heaven compared to hell, but it is hell compared to heaven.

God wants us to experience good and bad on earth and to realize that a far greater good and bad exists inside eternity when we arrive there. And we can thank the Lord that He shows us very clearly in His holy Word how we can make sure we will end up experiencing the greatest "good" with Him throughout eternity vs the worst "bad" without Him throughout eternity.

Amazingly, we are "all" destined to spend eternity separated from God because we are born spiritually dead forever with our sin nature, but He provides a WAY for us to go from being spiritually dead forever to being spiritually alive forever in order to spend eternity in the "good" place with Him vs the "bad" place without Him.

BACK TO GOD'S PLAN

Again, everything God creates He creates for His pleasure. And don't forget, it's relationships that bring God His most pleasure. It certainly seems at this point we human beings are not bringing God any relationship "pleasure." But the truth is we human beings are bringing God the "most pleasure" He's ever created, as you will soon see.

Since all humans are born with a sin nature, this means we are born anti-God. As I've mentioned, we actually are children of Satan vs God because of our sin nature due to God calling man's seed Satan's seed.

This also means we are born with a pride nature vs a love nature. A pride "nature" means that since we put ourselves first, this actually puts all human beings in "competition" with each other. We all must have "things" to survive and enjoy what we consider the pleasures of this world - money, power, sex, fame, things, etc. It is all about who has the "most" and having the "most" by human thinking means having "things" to bring us the most pleasure of what life on earth has to offer.

Have you noticed how everything important to the human race is "external" which is temporary and everything important to God is "internal" which is eternal?

The bible says it is better to give than to receive.

Acts 20:35 says "In everything I did, I showed you that by this kind of hard work we must help the weak, remembering the words Jesus Himself said: It is more blessed to give than to receive".

Receiving is "external" and giving is "internal".

SO WHAT'S THE BIG DEAL ABOUT SIN?

What do you think most of the world even thinks about sin? Not much. How many "religions" on earth even talk about sin and what it truly means? Only one that I know of - Christianity.

I earlier mentioned how God's "standard" is complete holiness, perfection and without sin. Anything less than His standard is sin. Sin simply means "missing the mark" and the mark is God's "standard".

To the world, having to measure up to God's standard of complete holiness, perfection and no sin is "ridiculous" to us. That's the way you think when you have a sin nature. The world does not particularly even look at sin as a big problem, but if they did, they would look at it from a human perspective vs God's perspective.

The human perspective says if we want to spend eternity with God we have to do it "ourselves" by being good, nice, doing more good deeds than bad, etc.

It's a works program. It's like putting your good deeds and bad deeds on a scale and just making sure your good deeds outweigh your bad deeds. The biggest problem with that is how can you ever "know" if your good deeds outweigh your bad deeds? Shouldn't you know that "BEFORE" you enter eternity?

Let's look at two extreme examples of the way the world looks at how to spend eternity with God in heaven. Someone like Hitler is so evil he will most definitely go to hell and someone as wonderful as Mother Teresa will most definitely go to heaven, right?

Is that true? Both are born spiritually dead and will stay that way no matter what they do on earth "if" they do not come to have a personal intimate relationship with God. The only way to reach heaven is to go from being spiritually dead forever to being spiritually alive forever and this can only happen when all of our sins are "REMOVED" forever, and the most "amazing" thing is what God had to do to accomplish that. So, let's talk about that.

HOW GOD DEALS WITH SIN

As we already know God created us human beings to have a personal intimate relationship with Him, but that is "impossible" due to our sin nature. Anytime God enters into ANY relationship with an individual or a nation such as Israel, in the Old Testament, the first thing that has to happen is to deal with the sin problem.

To do this God has set up what is called the law of "atonement" which is the only way that God will allow an "innocent sinless blood sacrifice" to occur to pay for the sins of another.

The way He did that with the nation of Israel is He set up an animal sacrificial system where millions of animals were sacrificed over 2000 years to "pay the price" for the sins of the people of Israel in order to maintain a personal relationship with Himself.

Only animals could accomplish this at that time because their blood is "sinless" blood. That's because animals are not created in God's image like humans are. Human blood could not do it because of our sin nature. But it has to be done over and over because animals are not laying down their lives for us out of "love".

God says in John 15:13 Greater love has no one than to lay down one's life to save another.

God was showing the people of Israel sin is something He will not tolerate. And there can be NO sin between God and anyone He has a personal relationship with.

GOD DOES NOT TOLERATE SIN

Let's talk about "tolerate". So, what does tolerate really mean? It means you have to put up with something you do not have the power to do anything about. Also, tolerance leads to "intolerance".

Two good examples are smokers and non-smokers. Nonsmokers used to have to tolerate smokers because they had no power to do anything about it. But in the 1960's and beyond when people became more "health" conscious, the tide changed and more and more people quit smoking. Then the non-smokers went from being tolerant of smokers to being intolerant of smokers to where smokers have to work hard these days to find a place to smoke.

The second example is believers vs non-believers. Nonbelievers used to have to tolerate believers because they did not have the power to change anything. But in the 1960's when God was thrown out of our schools, our government and many other places, the non-believers gained power and went from being tolerant of believers to being intolerant of believers for the past few decades.

It's all about "power!" So, who has the most power? This is obviously a rhetorical question. Creator God has "ALL" the power and thus does not have to tolerate sin or anything else for that matter. Non-believers say believers are intolerant because we say Jesus is the only way to God, but it is not us saying this. Jesus Himself in God's Word in the Bible says He is. In John 14:6 Jesus says,

"I am the way and the truth and the life.
No one comes to the Father except through Me."

This is why the world hates the one "true" God and takes it out on Christians.

Let's get back to Israel. Through animal sacrifices God was also showing Israel they needed a Savior's sacrifice to replace once and for all the animal sacrifices.

The so-called way of righteousness with the nation of Israel is called the LAW, and the only way to be saved was never to break even one of God's laws which was an impossible task. Thus, they had to keep doing animal sacrifices to pay for their sins and stay in a relationship with God. God allowed this type of relationship with Israel to last around 2000 very long years.

GOD SENDS JESUS

It was then that God the Father decided to provide a way to save the whole human race by sending His Son, Jesus, to earth to pay the price for our sins.

Jesus lovingly sacrificed His life on a cross to pay the price for the sins of mankind. By doing this, God chose to accept His Son's blood in exchange for the blood of animal sacrifices.

Remember, I pointed out that any time "anyone" wants to have a personal relationship with God their sin issue has to be dealt with first. This is exactly what Jesus did. He paid the price for our sins and gives us His righteousness so that we can now have a personal intimate relationship with God through Jesus.

For what reason did Jesus do this? Was it so everyone on earth is now saved and will go to heaven? Not hardly. He did it so everyone on earth who "recognizes" who Jesus is and what He's done to save us and who "desires" to know Him can now enter into an intimate personal relationship with Him and instantly go from being spiritually dead forever to being spiritually alive forever. This is referred to as being "born again."

WHAT DOES BORN AGAIN MEAN?

Just as Jesus died and was resurrected, being born again means we die to our old spiritual sinful lives and are born again to begin our new spiritual lives in Christ.

The Bible wants all born again Christians to also get baptized for two reasons: One, baptism is a "representation" of us dying to our old sinful life and being raised to our new sinless life through Christ.

Two, baptism is a "public" confession of our love and desire to have Jesus be our Lord and Savior. In Matthew 10:32 Jesus says:

"Whoever acknowledges Me before others I will also acknowledge before My Father in heaven."

Baptism is not mandatory to be saved but is desired by God to show "publicly" we now belong to Jesus. Jesus died on the cross between two thieves where one asked Jesus to save him and the other didn't. Jesus told the one who asked to be saved that he would be in paradise with Him that very day. Obviously, that thief was not baptized.

To be born again, we do this by first simply "desiring" to "know" God and to have a personal, intimate relationship with Him. To have this kind of relationship, we need to ask God to forgive us of our sins and invite Jesus to come into our lives to be our Lord and Savior and empower us to start living a life that serves and pleases Him.

We want to serve and please Him - not because we are trying to "earn" our way into heaven, but out of "gratitude" for who He is and what He's done to save us.

Jesus dying on a cross to pay the price of our sins means all those who are born again have had "all" of our sins removed - past, present and future. Once that occurs, we go from being spiritually dead forever to being spiritually alive forever because our sin issue was taken care of by Jesus. Jesus and Jesus "alone" takes away all our sins and this is why Jesus says "again" in John 14:6:

"I am the way and the truth and the life.
No one comes to the Father except through me".
No other "religion" can do this and they hate Christianity because of it.

WHY THE WORLD HATES CHRISTIANITY

So why do you think the world really does hate Christianity? There are at least two major reasons. One, Christianity is what the world considers a religion where you are responsible to God and have to obey Him, and they do not want to be "accountable" to or judged by God. They see Christianity as a bunch of DON'Ts.

Two, they think it is ridiculous Christianity says that to be saved all we have to do is believe in Jesus. They see this as a "license" to sin. One verse in the Bible they get this from is one of the most popular - John 3:16 which says:

"For God so loved the world that He gave His one and only Son that whoever believes in Him shall not perish but have eternal life."

I myself wish this verse was written differently because of the word "believes." Believes can sound too much like head knowledge. I used to see it that way. Even though I did not grow up going to church, I did believe Jesus died for our sins. Thus, I figured I would live my life my way and see Jesus in heaven because I did believe He died on a cross to save us.

But this was just head knowledge. I wish it was written "that whoever has a personal relationship with Jesus shall not perish but have eternal life."

HOLY SPIRIT POWER CHANGES US

The world is not seeing or understanding about the personal relationship part. Many, if not almost all religions, don't even think it is possible to have a "personal" relationship with God.

What they don't understand is when God's believers are born again, God Himself "changes our lives". Instead of having a license to sin, we no longer "want" to sin and feel bad and repent when we do.

The world doesn't understand how the Holy Spirit power of God in us can "change us" to be vastly different from our old pre-born again self. It's not our "words" that changes us. It is "God's power" in us that changes us when He enters us through Holy Spirit God.

In reading the New Testament, it's interesting to see how the Holy Spirit changed Paul from passionately wanting to persecute and kill Christians to pouring out his life to lead people to a saving faith in Jesus Christ. He went from wanting to kill all Christians to wanting everyone to BE a Christian. This same man went on to become the author of a large portion of the New Testament.

I'm sure we have all known people whose lives are 180 degrees different now after being born again than their old lives of habitual sins or maybe going from prison to become an evangelical pastor, etc. Many prisoners have done that. There are tons of examples like this.

But how does it happen? Do you think it happens automatically under their own strength? Not hardly. It happens because the Holy Spirit's power in them changes everything about the way they view life and life's priorities.

In Josh McDowell's book, *The Case for Christ*, he asks this question, "If you were put on trial for being a Christian, would there be enough evidence to convict you?" The bottom line is you "WILL" become significantly different when you love the Lord and seek after Him, and your life will be so much better in every way because of it.

Also, the sad reality is that if you ask people if they are ready to become a born again Christian, most will hesitate or say no because they equate becoming a Christian as having to give up all the "fun" in their life and if "all" their fun comes from "sin," I can see why they would hesitate.

The saddest thing they don't understand is God's FUN is far, far greater than man's fun. God's fun is internal, spiritual and eternal. Man's fun is external, non-spiritual and "very" temporary.

BENEFITS OF THE HOLY SPIRIT CHANGING US

Also, what the world can never understand is that God truly does change you and your life will change in a much more fulfilling way because you now have God's peace and relationship in your life.

Knowing you truly belong to the Lord is more valuable than winning a billion-dollar lottery. That thought should be a "no brainer" because if you tried to put a monetary value on eternal life with God vs eternal life separated from God, how much do you think it would be worth?

How much would you be willing to pay for eternal life with God vs eternal life separated from Him? How about all the money in the universe! Salvation is "priceless!" There is only one person who can afford to pay the price to be able to spend eternity with Jesus and that is Jesus Himself. His death on a cross was the "only price" that would free us from our sins in order to have a born again relationship with Him.

On Good Friday, Jesus became our "martyr" when He died and paid the price for our sins. But you cannot prove you paid the price for "anything" without a receipt. On Sunday morning after the crucifixion Jesus became our "Savior" when His "resurrection" was God's "receipt" back to Him saying, "I accept your payment in full, Son!"

But what else does the Holy Spirit living in us truly mean? In John 14:20 Jesus says to His disciples,

"On that day you will realize that I am in my Father and you are in me and I am in you".

That day begins the day we become "born again.

With the Holy Spirit in us we are now "connected" to God or we have become a small part of God.

Think of God as Windows and angels as Mac. Mac supports Windows but is not part of Windows.

Think of born again Christians as a Windows "upgrade." We are now a small part of God. This helps explain why the Bible says we shall rule over angels. They are not connected to God in this way.

First Corinthians 6:3 says,

"Do you not know we will judge angels?

We have more "rank" than them, if you will. But God is allowing us to be "connected" to Himself in a small way. Do you have any clue how incredible that is and what it truly means? Why would God do such a thing? Later I will explain it, and the answer will amaze you!

At the beginning of this book, I explained that it appears our relationship with God is not pleasing Him. Then I said you will be shocked to find out what He is really doing. As I just mentioned, God is sharing "Himself" with us for all eternity.

We will not know what this fully entails until we are with Him in heaven, but it's the most amazing thing He's ever done. And us being with Him appears to be much "sooner" than most think. More on that later when I explain end time prophecy.

Now, how does it benefit us here on earth to have Holy Spirit God living in us? One of the reasons God blesses His born again children with the Holy

Spirit is so we can now "know" the "things of God."

Who is it that knows the things of God? Only God Himself. What are the things of God? It is the things God wants us to know in order to be changed from people living a sinful life to people doing our best to live Godly lives to please and serve Him. The truth is we can't change our sinful lives by ourselves.

But with Holy Spirit God now residing in us, new things begin to occur that never occurred before. For instance, when we continue to do our previous sinful things like maybe getting drunk or telling lies or telling filthy jokes or watching pornography, etc., all of a sudden something different happens. We start "feeling bad" about that - feeling guilty. Why? We never felt bad or guilty about it before. Why now?

It's because the Holy Spirit in us is "convicting" us of our sin. Now, for the first time we feel guilty about it and so we confess it to the Lord and ask for His help to overcome this sin. Some sins are difficult to break and it is a matter of continuing to strive to overcome whatever sins it is and keep confessing them and asking the Lord again to help us overcome them. The Lord knows our heart and will help us until that sin or sins is behind us.

Another major way the Holy Spirit in us helps us is super important - helping us "understand" God's word in the

Bible.

I am a great example of this. As I previously stated, I hardly ever went to church growing up and knew very little about the Bible. I didn't even know the Bible was filled with prophecies - thousands of them. I knew Jesus had died for our sins and if you believe that you then go to heaven.

I did believe that and said, thanks, Jesus, I'll see you in heaven someday. Little did I know at that time that it is not a "head" belief that Jesus died for us that saves us but a "heart" belief and a desire to know Him, love Him and turn our lives over to Him, as I mentioned earlier.

PROPHECY

What brought me to the point of falling in love with Jesus was when, at the age of 34, I read Hal Lindsey's book, *The Late Great Planet Earth*, which discussed the thousands of prophecies in the Bible. Approximately one-third of the Bible is prophecies.

Prophecy is simply the future written in advance. Obviously, only God knows and can tell us the accurate future. To me, this was proof positive that everything about heaven, hell and Jesus is true, and I did not want to end up in hell. I asked God to forgive me of my sins, and I asked Jesus to be my Lord and Savior. This simple step has resulted in a growing relationship ever since.

I was astounded by all of the prophecies in the Bible. In fact, I don't feel I came to the Lord in faith alone, but more through "scientific proof" due to it being impossible to forecast thousands of future events in advance.

Dr. David Reagan, a world-famous prophecy teacher and evangelist once said there are around 300 prophecies about the first coming of Jesus in the Bible written 700 years before He was born and there are over 500 prophecies talking about His Second coming.

Dr. Reagan said the odds of predicting accurately only eight prophecies in the Bible about a person and events about their life would be like filling up the state of Texas with silver dollars and then fly over the state with one silver dollar that has an X on it, drop it from the plane, mix them all up and then choose one and have it be the one with the X on it.

Those are super incredible odds but that is only for 8 prophecies. Imagine the odds of forecasting thousands correctly. To me, it's pure scientific "proof." Actually, it is far MORE than scientific proof. Scientific proof is "possible". Predicting thousands of prophecies is "impossible" and "proves" only God alone can do it.

UNDERSTANDING THE BIBLE

But let's get back to understanding the Bible. When I was going to the University of Texas, which was 8 years before I knew the Lord, I heard they offered a New Testament course I could take that was an easy A type of course, and I needed an A for my grade point average.

So, I took the course, read the whole New Testament and it meant basically nothing to me. It was just another book and I made my "A". But when I started reading the Bible after becoming born again, the words simply "jumped off the page at me ." I was blown away by all the things God was showing me in His Word such as how everything began and how everything ends and His whole plan in between. Why do I understand it now when I never understood it before? Because the Holy Spirit in me is showing me God's truth. This is also why the Bible says in 1 Corinthians 2:4:

"The things of God are foolishness to the world."

And 1 Corinthians 2:14 states:

"But the natural man does not accept the things of the Spirit of God for they are foolishness to him and he is not able to understand them because they are spiritually discerned" (Berean Literal Bible)

Most of us know there is great controversy in interpreting the Bible. There are many liberal Bible scholars who don't believe the Bible is the infallible, inerrant word of God and do not believe in many of the miracles in the Bible such as the virgin birth or even Jesus' resurrection.

WHAT! How is that possible? Easy! They are not born again and do not have the Holy Spirit in them to show them God's truth. Even a brand new born again Christian who has only read the Bible for perhaps a week has more Bible "wisdom" than liberal Bible scholars because the new born again Christian "knows" the Bible is the true Word of God and that gives him/her God's wisdom that non-born again scholars can only dream of.

THE HOLY SPIRIT COMMUNICATES IN DIFFERENT WAYS

The Holy Spirit is also our line of communication to God and from God in terms of us sending Him our prayers and He sending us His blessings.

God speaks to His born again children in many ways - mainly when we read and study His word in the Bible which is called the LIVING Word of God. It's living because God sees to it we can read certain verses perhaps dozens of times and often God will show us something new we never saw before. It is His way of communicating to us.

He also speaks to us through circumstances. Perhaps we cannot pay our rent and a check mysteriously appears out of nowhere to cover the rent. The world calls that a coincidence, but born again Christians know it as a God-incidence

A great example of this occurred in my own life in 1996. I have never smoked even one cigarette due to not liking the smell of cigarettes, but in 1996 I was diagnosed with tongue cancer that had metastasized into my lymph glands.

One doctor said this was a severe stage 4 cancer. He said my chances of surviving the next five years were around ten percent. I told the doctor God was in charge of that and I wanted a second opinion.

My second doctor looked at my MRI and CAT scans and agreed this is serious. He did not like the other doctor giving me a "percentage" of survival but said he needed to remove the large tumor on the base of my tongue.

The first doctor said chemo was a waste of time for my tongue cancer and he wanted to operate immediately. The surgery meant I would lose most of the base of my tongue, my pharyngeal wall, my lymph nodes and they would have to take a flap out of my chest to attach to my tongue area.

It sounded horrible. The second doctor confirmed the seriousness of the surgery and said at his hospital they always tried two rounds of chemo first and if that did not work, then they would need to do that horrible surgery. My speech would never be the same nor my swallowing. My life would be very different from that point forward and not in a good way physically.

To begin my two rounds of chemo treatment I had to have a port put into my chest to receive the chemo. On the day I was to receive the port, I woke up and told the Lord I was not looking forward to going through this, but I put my life in His hands and whatever He decided was fine with me.

When the first doctor said my chances of survival for the next five years were ten percent, this may sound "crazy" but at first, I got a little excited but only in terms of I might be getting ready to enter my eternal home much sooner than I thought and nothing is better than that.

However, I had been married only a year and a half and I told the Lord I loved my life, I loved my wife and if it would be possible to continue to live, then that would be great. But if it was time to come Home, that would be great, too. It was most definitely a win-win situation.

On my bathroom sink, I had a Bible verse calendar where each day was written a new Bible verse. I asked the Lord to give me an encouraging verse that day I was getting the port. I tore off the page to reveal the new Bible verse and it was Jeremiah 17:14 which said "Heal me O Lord and I will be healed; save me and I will be saved for Thou art my praise." I looked at that verse and started crying. I got SUPER excited and told my wife to come see what God had just shown me.

Well, I hung my hat on that verse and was completely convinced God was going to heal me. I went through my two rounds of chemo and the new MRI showed the tumor had shrunk almost half but not nearly enough to avoid that horrible surgery.

I saw my doctor for a final check-up a week before my surgery on Feb 20th, 1996. The tumor was still there and nothing had changed. I told the doctor about my Bible verse and that the Lord was going to heal me. So, I said, "When you go in, take a tissue sample, but don't go whacking away on my tongue." He said he would do that if that's what he saw.

A week later I went in to have my surgery. The operation was to last around 10 hours and my life would never be the same. As I went under, I said, "Heal me, O Lord, and I shall be healed" and that was about as far as I got before I went under. Around four hours later the nurse began shaking me saying, "Mr. Cogburn, wake up, wake up. Your surgery went great. The doctor could not find "any" cancer.

The tumor had completely disappeared. The doctor did not remove "any" of my tongue but did remove twenty-one lymph nodes in my neck area just to be on the safe side.

He wanted me to go through thirty-seven days of chemo and radiation. I told him I was not sure of that because God had just healed me. So, I told him if he found any cancer cells in any of those twenty-one lymph nodes, then I would go through the chemo and radiation. The next day they found a "few" cancer cells in one of the lymph nodes. That was disappointing, so I agreed to go through the chemo and radiation.

Today, twenty-six years later, I am having some physical repercussions due to the radiation, but I am so thankful to the Lord for extending my life here on earth and allowing me to have a great life with my wife and walking with Him on my journey to my eternal Home and life with Him.

What happened was a "miracle." A large tumor doesn't normally disappear in a week. I was on two Christian radio programs giving my testimony of God's wonderful miracle in my life.

I believe my story is a great example of how God often speaks to us through circumstances. I was in a life- threatening situation and God used a Bible verse to speak to me in a way I could understand and "that" is the key.

It is so exciting for God's born again children to see and know God just spoke to them about something they've been praying about. This is something God does in different ways for different people, and He does it in a way that each person can "understand."

God also often speaks to us through our brothers and sisters in Christ. We might need God's help with something. We pray about it and someone comes and advises us with the perfect answer. But it's the Holy Spirit keeping us on the right path and enjoying a relationship with God that pleases Him.

COINCIDENCE VS GOD-INCIDENCE

Earlier I spoke about the difference between coincidence and God-incidence. For unbelievers there is no God-incidence - only coincidence. Let's look at a couple of so called coincidences that are so HUGE just about everyone should call these God-incidences.

A few years ago, I was listening to Chuck Missler, a very well known evangelist and Bible scholar as well as a scientific scholar - a truly gifted and blessed man of God who is now residing in God's presence in heaven.

Chuck wrote an article about names in the Bible and their meaning. In the Hebrew language, names have meanings. For instance, the name Jesus means Savior. Chuck's article described the first 12 names in Genesis and what they mean.

Adam means <u>man</u>. Seth, Adam and Eve's second son means <u>appointed</u>. Enosh, Seth's son's name means <u>mortal, frail or miserable</u>. Kenan is Enosh's son and his name means <u>sorrow</u>.

Kenan's son is Mahalalel which means <u>blessed or praise,</u> and the El in his name is the name of God. Thus, Mahalalel means the <u>blessed God</u>. Another Hebrew name that includes El, the name of God is Dan-i-EL, which means, <u>God is my judge</u>.

Mahalalel's son is Jared and his name means <u>shall come down</u>. Jared's son is Enoch which means <u>teaching or commencement</u>. Enoch was the father of Methuselah and his name broken out means <u>his death shall bring</u>. Methuselah's son is Lamech which means <u>despairing</u>, and Lamech is the father of Noah which means <u>rest or comfort.</u>

When you put together the meaning of these 12 names it reads like this: Man (is) appointed mortal sorrow; (but) the Blessed God shall come down teaching (that) His death shall bring (the) despairing rest.

This is the gospel hidden within the genealogy of Genesis. How amazing and God-incidental is that? If you would like to read Chuck's full article, it is at

khouse.org/articles/1996/44

Let me share one more God-incidence. What is the middle verse in the Bible? There are 929 chapters in the Old Testament and 260 chapters in the New Testament for a total of 1189 chapters. The middle chapter of the Bible is Psalms 118 and the middle verse in the Bible is Psalms 118:9 which lines up perfectly with the 1189 chapters in the Bible. And what does the middle verse of Psalms 118:9 say?

"It is better to put your trust in the Lord than your confidence in man".

Do you think that's a coincidence? Not hardly.

Now hopefully no one will find "these" to be a coincidence but plainly God-incidences. There are so many of these in the Bible that someone could probably write a book on them alone.

MORE BENEFITS OF THE HOLY SPIRIT IN US

Another "biggie" that the Holy Spirit does for us is give us God's "peace, joy and contentment." These have zero to do with money and/or tangible things.

It is sad that so-called prosperity ministers try to convince us that if we have enough faith God will be like our personal genie and give us everything we desire. They misinterpret God's word by pointing out the Bible says whatever we ask for we shall receive and that certainly makes God look like a genie. That would actually put us in control. But what it really means is that whatever we ask for "in God's will" we will receive. That shows God is always in control.

The perfect example of this is right before Jesus was arrested to be crucified. He was praying in the garden of Gethsemane and said, "Father, if you are willing, take this cup (crucifixion) from me, yet not my will but yours be done."

And so, anything we pray for, whether it be to save a loved one from cancer or for a new job, we should pray "knowing" God's answer is always the right answer whether we understand it or not. God wants us to trust Him in all things.

GOD'S PEACE, JOY AND CONTENTMENT

God's peace is the only "true" peace because it is an "internal eternal peace." God's peace takes away the number one fear of this world - "death."

Why is death the number one fear of this world? The world fears what it does not understand, and it sees death as the end of all things. When you sense danger you have fear because you don't know what is going to happen and it might be bad.

When you belong only to this world you can't see beyond it. It is like that old saying - eat, drink and be merry for tomorrow we die or like that old beer commercial - you only go around once in life so you've got to grab for all the gusto you can.

What is the main difference between the world and born again Christians? We have God's internal, eternal "peace." This means we have zero fear of death because we know "true life" is eternity with God living in His presence which "begins" at death or the rapture, whichever comes first.

For the world, death is the end. For born again Christians, death is our eternal "beginning." (The rapture will be explained later.)

God's peace also brings true contentment. It is the type of peace that the world can never understand. Why is contentment difficult for the world? It's because the world is about "more, more, more!" It is all about competition.

What causes this? Comparing! When you look at what others have compared to what you have and that's important to you, then you have "discontentment".

God's contentment eliminates "comparing" that produces discontentment. But if you "are comparing at all, you are happy for those who have more and you are not in competition to equal or exceed them. I came up with a bumper sticker slogan years ago that says it all:

"Try contentment. You will not find it "wanting."

So, when you know you belong to the Lord, you are perfectly satisfied with everything God is doing in your life. You are not jealous over others who may have more than you. You are not comparing your life to others lives. You are enjoying the Lord and His blessings and the things you are doing in your life to serve and please Him.

What He gives us is far "greater" than what we give Him.

This type of peace and contentment is far different than worldly peace and contentment which is often lacking. The rich are often looking for more wealth and are not fully content until they have it. For many of them, life is about who has the "most things" because after all, isn't having more "things" what life is about here on earth?

And don't get me wrong. God does bless many born again Christians financially who are very wealthy and have lots of "things," but the big difference is they "know" everything they have is a blessing from God and actually "belongs" to God. Thus, they want to be a good steward with God's provisions.

GOD'S JOY

Another eternal blessing from God is joy. One of our favorite Christmas songs is, "Joy to the World." If you turn joy into an acronym it describes how God desires us to view relationships in priority order from His perspective:

J for Jesus
O for others
Y for you

Joy is God's "happiness" bestowed upon us. God's joy is different from the world's joy and happiness. God's joy is internal happiness from God, while the world sees no difference between joy and happiness.

We all want happiness, but worldly happiness is more "external" than internal. God's joy produces our "internal" joy and happiness for one main reason. We belong to Him and are His children. Nothing but nothing is more "important" than that.

The Bible says when we become born again we become a new "creature." We no longer belong to this temporary world but belong to God and His eternal world.

Without the Holy Spirit all of this sounds ridiculous to the world. Without the Holy Spirit the world and human lifespan is its "focus." With the Holy Spirit, heaven and "eternity" is its focus. Which one do you think is more important? I hope that is another rhetorical question.

WHAT IS THE "SOURCE" OF OUR BELIEFS?

I spoke a little about this earlier, but this section is of "major" importance because it is where the rubber meets the road in terms of "knowing" what is the "truth" about knowing God and how to spend eternity with Him.

There have been hundreds if not thousands of different religions and/or beliefs ever since the beginning of mankind. Remember that we all have a sin nature. As a result, we are born anti-God. However, God has built into all of us the ability to know He is real. And even though He is invisible, He shows His invisibility in a way that leaves everyone without excuse. In fact, Romans 1:20 KJV says,

"For the invisible things of Him (God) from the creation of the world are clearly seen, being understood by the things that are made, even His eternal power and Godhead so that they are without excuse."

In other words, His designed "creation" shows us that only "His power" can create the universe and all life on planet earth and no one can tell Him, "I didn't know you existed."

However, the irony is, because of this instinct God puts in humans to see Him, mankind has "always" desired to worship "something" much greater than ourselves.

But the problem is many miss the mark because they end up worshiping "created things" instead of the Creator. They have worshiped the sun, the moon, the Greek gods like Zeus and his gang and many more created things. Some religions worship many different things they call gods. If you like lots of gods, check out Hinduism.

Why do you think they want to worship "created things" instead of the Creator Himself? They "want" to worship a higher "something" but they don't want to worship a higher something that judges them and holds them accountable.

The sun, moon and all created things do not judge us but the Creator of all things holds us accountable and does judge us. Therefore, we don't seek Him out with our sin nature and we try to avoid Him as much as possible.

Of course, I am speaking of the world and not people who actually do see the "visible" Creator God and "want" to know Him and worship Him.

Because there are hundreds of religions and beliefs, don't you think it is important to find out which one or ones is correct or do you just assume all of them are correct?

We hear all the time there are MANY ways to God. From a worldly point of view that just makes sense, doesn't it?

Oprah Winfrey and many celebrities believe this. But why? It is because they think it is ludicrous that there could be only one way to God when the majority of the world does not believe that. They don't believe that a "loving" God would send anyone to hell just because they believe a different way than Christianity.

This is New Age thinking. I came up with another bumper sticker slogan that describes this perfectly:

"God created man in His own image. New Age is man's attempt to return the favor."

And that is what they do - try to create God in OUR image. They are looking at God from "our" perspective vs "His" perspective.

To understand God's truth, we need to examine the "source" of our beliefs. I think it is safe to say most people believe the way they do about God because they are "born" into that belief system and culture. It makes it more difficult if you are born into a "false" belief system and grow up with those beliefs and then hear later that Christianity says that Jesus says no one comes to the Father except through Him.

Jesus is saying that all other belief systems except Christianity are "wrong" and are on their way to hell. WOW, that is one heavy duty statement and truth. No wonder the world hates Christianity.

But is it the truth? Just because Jesus says it, does that mean He's right when He says He is the only way to the Father? How can we verify this?

We need to understand the source of our beliefs. For some like the Muslims, the Hindus, the Jews and the Mormons, they have their own Bible or beliefs in written form.

The Muslims have the Koran, the Hindus have the Veda, the Mormons have the Book of Mormon and the Jewish people have the Old Testament. We Christians have the Bible which is the only one where "all of it" is called the Word of God. The Jewish people only call the Old Testament the Word of God while Christians have the Old and New Testament.

These are only five examples of people that have some sort of written source for their beliefs. Of these five, the Jewish people are the closest to Christianity because the Jewish people wrote most of the Bible, Old and New Testament, but most of them do not recognize the New Testament as the Word of God and Jesus as their Messiah yet. That means they, too, cannot come to the Father if they don't come through Jesus.

GOD'S "PROOF" OF THE TRUTH OF HIS WORD

Okay, let's nail this down. Christianity says they are the only truth to God since they are quoting Jesus. PROVE IT! Is there anything different about the Bible compared to all other religions in the world? The answer is a big time YES!

How so? Thousands of prophecies that I spoke of earlier. Again, prophecy is the future written in advance. Do we know of anyone on earth who can predict thousands of future events and never be wrong? And no, Nostradamus and people like him do not even come close. It should be "obvious" that only God can.

Again, approximately "one-third" of the Bible is filled with prophecy. Why do you think that is? It is because God "knew" since He is invisible most people would be skeptical of "anyone" saying they are the only way to God.

And thus, when God inspires different authors to write "His" Word of God book, He needs to make it a "Supernatural" book written by men who are Inspired by God vs a natural book written by man alone. In Isaiah 46:10 God says,

"I alone am God and make known the end from the beginning. I shall accomplish all that I please."

The Bible is the only book in the entire world that has thousands of "accurate" future events written for us in advance. It is saying WAKE UP! Can any other religion or anyone else write the future in advance? Dwell on that fact and reality! Let it be "important" to you!

Amazingly, most of the world completely "ignores" all the prophecies in the Bible as if they are no big deal. This is like there is going to be a 100-mile race between all religions and Christianity. There will be only one winner who gets to spend eternity with God. All religions will be riding their bicycles during this race while Christianity will be driving its Lamborghini. And all the religions are ignoring the Lamborghini, thinking they will win the race with their bicycles.

The most "important" future events from the beginning are the first and second coming of Jesus. Again, there are over 300 prophecies written in the Old Testament about the first coming of Jesus and over 500 about the second coming of Jesus and all were written 700 years before Jesus was born.

How can anyone or any religion completely ignore the most important EVIDENCE there is to prove the Bible is the true Word of God? This evidence should cause "everyone" who desires the truth to at least investigate and "compare" to their own faith or any other faith for verification.

ISRAEL IN PROPHECY

God tells us in the Old Testament the nation of Israel will disobey Him and be exiled all over the earth. No longer will they be a nation because of their sin and especially because they were responsible for putting Jesus on the cross.

For almost 2000 years Israel no longer existed as a nation, but the Bible also says in the end times God will restore the Jewish people back to their homeland Israel in ONE DAY and He will revive their dead language.

Isaiah 66:8 says "Who has heard such things? Who has seen such things? Shall a land be born in one day? Shall a nation be brought forth in one moment"?

This occurred on May 14, 1948 when Israel came back to life to be a nation again. No other nation in history has ever been destroyed and then restored sometime in the future. They also spoke many different languages when they came back to Israel, but changed back to ancient Hebrew which they speak today just as God prophesied they would thousands of years ago.

Zephaniah 3:9 (God is talking about Israel's restoration):

For at that time, I will change the speech of the peoples to a pure speech that all of them may call upon the name of the Lord and serve Him with one accord.

The pure speech is referring to ancient Hebrew the Jewish people spoke before their nation was destroyed.

Restoring Israel to be a nation again was God's greatest miracle for the 20th century and many of us older folks got to witness it even though many of us were babies at that time.

God also tells us Jesus is coming back for His second coming and He is going to take over the planet and rule it for 1000 years. But let me stop there because I want to save the end time events for later. You get the idea. God can and does tell us the future and He has never been wrong. As to all future events in the Bible that have not occurred yet, it is not a matter of IF they will occur, but WHEN they will occur.

GOD'S PROPHECY VS MAN'S THINKING

Here is a good "earthly" example of the importance of prophecy. Let's pretend there is a man who says only he can predict all the lottery numbers accurately and each week there is a 25-

million-dollar lottery. And let's say he predicts the winning lottery numbers "in order" for 1000 times in a row.

Do you think you would be saying for the next lottery, "I don't believe he can do that again so I am going to guess my own numbers?" Or do you think you would play his numbers? That is also a rhetorical question.

Obviously, it would be incredible if someone actually could do that, but even "that" example "pales" in comparison to what God has actually done for us in the Bible with His thousands of prophecies concerning people, nations, events, the future, etc.

The odds of this happening are way beyond the possibility stage, and this should be proof "ENOUGH" for anyone to see and understand the Bible "alone" is a Supernatural book from God. And what Jesus says about how no one comes to the Father except through Him is, indeed, true.

HOW GOD'S INFLUENCE CHANGES THINGS

Here's another question. Do you really think God could physically come into our world or write a book to our world and not have it change the world forever?

All of "time" changed because of the birth of Jesus. No one on earth has "ever" impacted our planet like Jesus. Do you think if God writes a book it will be a best seller? Google it and you will find the Bible has sold at least 5 "billion" copies and is the best seller each and every year. Second place is the Koran with 800 million copies and third is the book of Mormon with 120 million copies.

With the Bible proving itself to be the only Supernatural book on the planet and Jesus saying no one comes to the Father except through Him, I hope and pray anyone reading this book will set aside their own biases and look "objectively" at everything I have pointed out so far.

Hopefully, "all" of us are searching for the "truth" about how to "know" God and spend eternity with Him. We don't want to make a mistake because that would be the worst "eternal" mistake possible. Fortunately, God makes it so easy for us to know the truth through His prophecy filled Word of God Bible.

CONSEQUENCES OF MAKING THE RIGHT DECISION

There is no doubt it is harder to have been born into a different religion and then be told at some point your religion is "wrong" compared to those who are born into the Christian faith. However, even most of them still do not believe the Bible due to the sin nature in all of us.

But, since Jesus says no one comes to the Father except through Him and the Bible proves it is the true word of God, "please" examine this carefully. For, there is "nothing" more important than spending eternity with God in heaven vs spending eternity separated from God. I have said this several times, and it is so important it can never be said enough.

Remember I said the theme of this book is relationship and the most important relationship for all of us is a relationship with God. Even common sense should be yelling at us God created us "because" He wants a personal intimate relationship with each of us.

I will talk about the "intimate" part later. He loves us and wants us to love Him back with our free will and once we fully understand who Jesus is and what He has done to save us from our sins in order to make that happen, it should make our love for Him jump off the charts.

THE BIBLE

If you knew 100 percent that God Himself sent you a letter and it is in your mailbox, would you read it? I think the vast majority of us would quickly read it. The Bible IS that letter! A long letter for sure but still God's "love" letter to the world showing us His love for us and desiring our love back.

I have already shown how the Bible is the verifiable Word of God. I have also shown how it is the number one bestseller of all times and also the best seller each and every year and the irony is it is the best seller of all times from people who have a sin nature.

REASONS PEOPLE IGNORE THE BIBLE

With that being the case why don't more people read and study the Bible? There are several reasons. Many people consider it way too long, too complicated, too hard to understand, too boring, too many interpretations and thus, have no interest in reading it. Most also say "where do you begin - at the beginning in the Old Testament or should you skip to the New Testament. How do you get started?

I mentioned earlier how some people turn the word Bible into an acronym that stands for Basic Instructions Before Leaving Earth and it does not get any more perfect than that since it is Creator God who is giving us those instructions.

Again, God tells us how everything began, how everything ends and just about everything else we need to know in between to live the very best life possible if we "follow" His instructions. The biggest problem is most people do not view the Bible that way at all. They certainly do not see it as the true word of God and His instructions for how to live life on earth.

One of my strongest desires and prayer is that many of you who read this book and do not know the Lord or much of the Bible will start to realize how different, how important and how Supernatural the Bible really is and how this new information might cause you to start thinking about God, eternity with Him and His Bible in a totally different way.

At the end of this book, I will explain everything anyone needs to know on how to personally and intimately know Jesus and belong to Him now and forever as well as how to get started with your new born again life in Him. But hang in there because there are still more fascinating parts of God's plan I want to show you.

GOD'S 7000 YEAR TIME PLAN BROKEN DOWN

Many theologians and the Jewish Talmud say God's plan for human beings has a beginning and an end and that time frame is 7000 years.

How do we know this? The Bible concerning earth begins with Genesis and begins with God explaining how He created everything concerning the universe and earth. He tells us He created everything in seven days which consisted of six days of work and one day of rest.

Seven in the Bible is God's "perfect" number. It is the number of "completion" and the Bible is replete with the number seven.

The Bible also says in 2 Peter 3:8 and Psalm 90:4 that a day with God is as 1000 years. God told Adam and Eve on the "day" they ate of the forbidden fruit they would die. This did not mean the very day they ate they would die but they would die within God's day of 1000 years and the oldest human to ever live is Methuselah who lived to be 969 years - just 31 years from God's 1000 year day.

God's plan includes the first 2000 years under no law, the second 2000 years under the law through Israel and the third 2000 years under grace through Jesus called the church age.

Those are six 1000 years of WORK - man being here on earth running things vs God running things. The 7th day of REST of 1000 years is when

God Jesus comes back to set up His millennial reign and rule the planet.

Earth will be governed under the Theocracy of Jesus Christ. He and all of His saints will be here running the planet. During that time only human beings who became believers during the 7-year tribulation, which I will talk about, will be allowed to enter into Jesus' 1000-year millennial reign and we "new saints" will be here to help govern the planet. More on the 7-year tribulation later.

JESUS' 1000-YEAR MILLENNIAL REIGN

Human beings will coexist at that time alongside Jesus and all His saints "visibly."

Isaiah 65:20 says "never again will there be in it an infant who lives but a few days or an old man who does not live out his years. The one who dies at a hundred will be thought to be a mere child. The one who fails to reach a hundred will be considered accursed.

During this 1000-year time frame the earth shall be restored to how it was at the beginning with people living again up toward 1000 years. Still, no one will reach 1000 because God does not allow any human being to live more than a 1000- year day which is okay since Jesus' day of rest itself is also 1000 years to complete God's 7000-year plan for human beings.

Isaiah 11:6-9 talks about during this 1000-year day of rest that the wolf shall live with the lamb, the lion shall eat straw like the ox, the nursing child shall play with the snake, etc., along with much longer life spans. The earth is changed to be more like it was at the beginning but this is not when God makes a new heavens and a new earth. That comes later.

END TIME PROPHECY IS NOW DURING "OUR" LIFETIME

We are living in a very precarious time right now on planet earth. Many people - both believers and non-believers alike are saying we are living in the end times.

What is the end times? End of what? For believers it is the end right before Jesus comes back for His 2nd coming and takes over the planet. For unbelievers, they see it as what they call the "apocalypse" which to them means the possible end of the earth and mankind and not the 2nd coming of Jesus. The irony is the Google definition of "apocalypse" is the complete final destruction of the world as described in the book of Revelation. They will, indeed, say the apocalypse has arrived when the 7-year tribulation begins and they will be "right".

There is no question the end times is a time leading "up to" this horrible destruction which will 100 percent occur. How do we know? Again, 100 percent verifiable Bible prophecy.

The book of Revelation refers to this time as a 7-year tribulation during which God pours out His wrath on mankind for its sins and also to finally bring the nation of Israel and the Jewish people to the truth that Jesus Christ "is" their long-awaited Messiah whom they have been waiting 4000 years for since they did not recognize Him as their Messiah when He was here the first time 2000 years ago.

But when can we truly "expect" His coming? Could the end of the age actually be in OUR lifetime? After all, people have been watching for Jesus to return for 2000 years. What is different "now" compared to the past 2000 years? Is there anything in God's prophecies that might narrow down when Jesus' 2nd coming might occur?

The good news is there is a "lot" of information in God's prophecies concerning when this time is most likely to occur. So, let's delve into it.

EVIDENCE THAT THE END TIMES IS IN OUR LIFETIME

Let's begin with Hosea 5:15 through 6:3. God is speaking to

Israel and in Hosea 5:15 God says to them:

"I will go and return to my place". (God is talking about the future when Jesus has paid the price for our sins and has returned back to Heaven). "I will go and return to my place until they (Israel) acknowledge their offense

(Crucifying and rejecting Jesus) and seek My face."

Zechariah tells us at the end of the 7-year tribulation Israel will finally recognize Jesus as their long-awaited Messiah and will call on Him to save them at the battle of Armageddon, which He does at His 2nd coming.

Hosea 6:1-3 continues: Now Israel is speaking -

"Come, let us return unto the Lord for He hath torn and He will heal us, He hath smitten and He will bind us up. After 2 days (2 of God's 1000-year days) He will revive us so that on the 3rd day we may live in His presence."

To be revived means you have to be dead first and God is saying He will revive dead Israel after 2000 years. Why? So, that on the 3rd 1000 years they (Israel) may live in His presence.

This 1000 years is Jesus' 1000-year millennial reign on earth. Israel and all believers are living in His presence at that time along with all of His saints who came back with Him for His 2nd coming to rule planet earth.

We know Israel was destroyed as a nation in 70 AD when the Romans destroyed Jerusalem and the temple and dispersed the Jewish people all over the planet. Israel ceased to exist as a nation until May 14, 1948 when God resurrected them to be a nation once again like He promised several times in the Old Testament. Israel is and always has been the "key" to not only all prophecy, but especially end time prophecy which "begins" with Israel coming back to life in 1948.

How do we know that? Easy! In Matthew 24 Jesus Himself tells us the GENERATION that will see His coming and the end of the age along with all the major signs preceding it. This is so important I will quote the scripture vs just summarizing it.

Matt 24:1 (NIV). This passage deals with Jesus being in

Jerusalem right before His crucifixion and He is talking with His disciples on the Mount of Olives and here is the conversation: "Jesus left the temple and was walking away when His disciples came up to Him to call His attention to its buildings.

"Do you see all these things, He asked? Truly I tell you not one stone here will be left on another. Every single one will be thrown down."

(This happened about 40 years later when Titus and the Romans destroyed Jerusalem and the temple. They threw down all of the stones because the temple was involved in a fire and there was gold in the temple structure and the fire melted the gold. The Romans then tore it apart stone by stone to get to the gold, thus, fulfilling Jesus' prophecy.

Matt 24:3 "As Jesus was sitting on the Mount of Olives, the disciples came to Him privately. Tell us, they said, when will this happen and what will be the sign of your coming and of the end of the age?"

(The disciples asked "point blank" what is the sign of your coming and of the end of the age?) You cannot get more direct than that and the good news is Jesus "does" answer this question.

Matt 24:4 "Jesus answered: Watch out that no one deceives you. For many will come in my name claiming, "I am the Messiah" and will deceive many. You will hear of wars and rumors of wars but see to it that you are not alarmed. Such things must happen, but the end is still to come. Nation will rise against nation and kingdom against kingdom. There will be famines and earthquakes in various places. All of these are the beginning of <u>birth pains.</u>

(Jesus uses the analogy of birth pains in that when a mother starts to feel birth pains leading up to the birth of her baby, those pains will increase in frequency and intensity up until the time of the birth.)

"Then you will be handed over to be persecuted and put to death and you will be hated by all nations because of Me. At that time many will turn away from the faith and will betray and hate each other and many false prophets will appear and deceive many people. Because of the increase of wickedness, the love of most will grow cold, but the one who stands firm to the end will be saved. And this gospel of the kingdom will be preached in the whole world as a testimony to all nations and then the end will come.

So, when you see standing in the holy place the abomination that causes desolation spoken of through the prophet Daniel, then let those who are in Judea flee to the mountains. Let no one on the housetop go down to take anything out of the house. Let no one in the field go back to get their cloak. How dreadful it will be in those days for pregnant women and nursing mothers!

Pray that your flight will not take place in winter or on the Sabbath. For then there will be great distress, unequaled from the beginning of the world until now and never to be equaled again. If those days had not been cut short, no one would survive, but for the sake of the elect those days will be shortened.

At that time if anyone says to you "look, here is the Messiah or there he is, do not believe it. Or false messiahs and false prophets will appear and perform great signs and wonders to deceive, if possible, even the elect. See, I have told you ahead of time.

So, if anyone tells you, there he is out in the wilderness, do not go out or here he is in the inner rooms, do not believe it. For as lightning that comes from the east is visible even in the west, so will be the coming of the Son of Man. (Jesus' 2nd coming will be from the East to

Jerusalem.)

Wherever there is a carcass, there the vultures will gather. Immediately after the distress of those days the sun will be darkened, and the moon will not give its light. The stars will fall from the sky and the heavenly bodies will be shaken.

Then will appear the sign of the Son of Man in heaven. And then all the peoples of the earth will mourn when they see the Son of Man coming on the clouds of heaven with power and great glory. And He will send His angels with a loud trumpet call and they will gather His elect from the four winds, from one end of the heavens to the other".

Most people don't get too excited about all of these "signs" Jesus just enumerated like wars and famines and earthquakes, etc., because they say these signs have always occurred.

So, what's the big deal about these signs? First, Jesus says these signs will increase in frequency and intensity during this time and then He tells us WHEN the end time events will BEGIN. (Verse 32 narrows down the time frame for His 2nd coming)

"Now learn the lesson from the fig tree."

(In the Old Testament, God often refers to the nation of Israel as a fig tree. When Jesus and His disciples were on their way to Jerusalem, they passed a fig tree that did not have any fruit on it, only leaves, and it was the time of year it should be showing some fruit. When Jesus saw the fig tree had no fruit on it, He put a curse on it and it withered and died.

(Matt 21:18-22) Jesus is getting ready to now answer His disciples' question about when will these signs and the end of the age be.

NARROWING DOWN THE END TIME TO A GENERATION

Matt 24: 32-35 Jesus says "now learn the lesson from the fig tree: As soon as its twigs get tender and its leaves come out, you know that summer is near. Even so, when you see all of these things (the signs that Jesus just told them) you know that it is near, right at the door. Truly I tell you, "THIS GENERATION" will certainly not pass away until all these things have happened. Heaven and earth will pass away but my Words will never pass away".

What Jesus just told the disciples as to the timing of His 2nd coming and the end of the age is that the generation that sees the fig tree (Israel) come back to life would be the generation that will see His 2nd coming and the end of the age.

The fig tree Israel came back to life on May 14, 1948. So, how long is a generation in the Bible?

Some will debate that but Psalm 90:10 defines a generation as either 70 years or 80 years with strength. 70 years from 1948 was 2018 and 80 years is 2028. Actually, it is 2018-19 and 2028-29 because the Bible uses a Hebrew calendar when calculating time and the new year on a Jewish calendar is always either in September or October.

If you add in the 0 year between BC and AD it could extend it to 2030 which some ascribe to. The book of Revelation tells us that Jesus' 2nd coming occurs right "after" the 7-year tribulation period.

So, we know that the 7-year tribulation period ends with Jesus' 2nd coming. From a math standpoint an 80-year generation from the fig tree Israel coming back to life is 2028-2030 MINUS 7 years for the 7-year tribulation which ends up being 2022-2023. This is saying that it is possible the 7-year tribulation could begin sometime this year or next.

EXPLAINING WHAT THE RAPTURE IS

But WAIT, there is something I have to talk about now in terms of "timing". It is the rapture of the church. I am not sure how many people who read this book will even know what the rapture is. We all have heard about the 2nd coming of Jesus someday but not everyone knows that Jesus comes "FIRST" for His bride the church and takes us back to heaven with Him and this occurs "before" the 7-year tribulation begins.

I will go into depth on what the rapture is all about later. But Jesus coming back for His bride occurs only in the "air" and He does not come back to earth to begin His 1000- year millennial reign until the 7-year tribulation ends. His 2nd coming actually "ends" it.

The most amazing part of this from a "timing" standpoint is that if the 7-year tribulation is to begin sometime this year or next, the rapture occurs "before" the 7-year tribulation even begins.

Now I am "not" a date setter. Most of us have heard of the very popular verse in the Bible where Jesus says no one knows the exact day or hour of His coming - not the angels or even Himself - but only the Father knows. This is not talking about His 2nd coming but only about His coming for His bride the church as you will see later.

"NOW" IS THE TIME TO ACT

One of the main purposes of this book is to show you how we can have a personal intimate relationship with God and live forever with Him and how the Bible is the true verifiable Word of God through thousands of fulfilled prophecies.

It is also to show you that Jesus' 2nd coming and especially Him coming for His bride the church, who is all born again Christians, is something that is so close it could actually happen in a matter of weeks or months.

AVOID THE 7-YEAR TRIBULATION

The BEST thing that can happen to any person on the planet right now is to enter into a personal intimate relationship with God through Jesus by being born again through repentance and asking Jesus to come into your life to be your Lord and Savior.

By doing so you will go "with" Jesus when He comes for His bride the church and ALL of us born again Christians will already be in "heaven" when the 7-year tribulation begins.

This is when God pours out His wrath on planet earth.

The church goes through the 7-year tribulation in heaven for the wedding celebration while everyone else goes through a hell on earth type of judgment during the 7-year tribulation during God's wrath poured out for all the sins of mankind.

God's prophecy tells us that it will be the worst time ever to be alive on earth during this time. And I just quoted Jesus above in Matt 24 where Jesus says that if those days were not shortened, no life on earth could survive. He is saying that if God did not step in and stop this, all life would be destroyed.

The book of Revelation tells us that around one-half of the population of earth will die during this 7-year period. That is over three BILLION people dying in seven years. And don't forget - this is not guess-work or a "maybe". It is God's never wrong accurate prophecy of what "will occur" and apparently very soon.

The end time scenario heading into the 7-year tribulation period will be "following" the rapture.

Think of the tribulation as being a giant snowball sitting at the top of a mountain with the rapture being the event that pushes it to start rolling down the mountain.

There will be a short time between the rapture and the beginning of the 7-year tribulation. Daniel 9:27 tells us that the tribulation "begins" when a one world leader called the antichrist signs a 7-year peace treaty with Israel and that is something everyone who is still here can watch for.

The world will NEVER be the same after an event like the rapture where God in an instant removes perhaps as many as one billion people off the planet who are born again Christians.

Do you think the world will go into chaos when such an event occurs? You bet they will. Do you think the "world" will be saying, "oh, darn, we missed the rapture?" Not hardly. The world will think they are the "lucky ones" because they did not disappear and are still here. Little do they know they are the "unlucky ones" and what is about to befall them.

WHO GOES AT THE RAPTURE AND WHAT HAPPENS FOLLOWING IT?

Here is what is interesting. When it comes to which countries in the world will lose the most born again Christians at the rapture, who do you think that will be? The USA will certainly be in the top of the list in terms of numbers of people who disappear due to our evangelistic work for sharing the gospel with the rest of the world.

The number of people who attend church in Europe has dropped precipitously over the past few decades and thus they will not lose as many people in the rapture.

But let me say something very "important" here. Attending church is NOT what saves you. It's that personal intimate relationship with Jesus that saves people whether they attend church or don't attend church.

I think it is safe to say that the number of people who attend church and still miss the rapture is, unfortunately, greater than we might imagine.

However, God wants born again believers to attend church and so we, obviously, can "expect" that there will be far more born again believers in church than non-born again believers, whether they go to church or not.

When I say it appears there are less people in Europe going to church than the USA, that usually means the number of "born again" believers will be less.

When you look at the major powers in the world, we can know that Russia and China will probably lose less than the USA in their population and the same is true for the Middle East. Israel and all the Arab countries will lose a tiny fraction of their people.

But the world will be in chaos from the standpoint of WHAT JUST HAPPENED!!! This is CRAZY! Where did all those people go??? The world will try to explain it away by something other than a rapture of born again Christians where God is saying in a HUGE WAY, "I will take you people and I don't want the rest of you".

Those taken are heaven bound and those left behind are hell bound "at that MOMENT" The GOOD NEWS is those left behind still have a 2nd CHANCE to come to know the Lord during the 7-year tribulation and be saved to be with Him for all eternity. It won't be a fun time but SALVATION is the only thing that matters so let's talk about that.

CAN PEOPLE BE SAVED FOLLOWING THE RAPTURE?

As I just mentioned, at the very "moment" the rapture occurs there will not be one born again Christian left alive on earth. BUT we can know that there are tons of people who do know about the rapture now and many will think they should have been raptured also but are left behind - just like was demonstrated by the very popular book series "Left Behind" written by Tim LeHaye and Jerry Jenkins.

They showed this happening and these people will quickly repent and turn to the Lord to be their Lord and Savior as well as millions more who start learning about all of this and this should create, hopefully, the largest revival the planet has ever known.

I also hope this book will still be around following the rapture and the truth of the rapture happening should cause many people to seriously pay attention to everything written in this book.

There is debate among some Christians who say that if you are not saved before the rapture then you will not be saved after the rapture during the tribulation. I personally disagree with that because millions of people who thought they were Christians but who were left behind will instantly KNOW they were "not" saved when they wanted to be and thought they were.

The rapture will show them they were wrong and many of them will repent and turn their lives over to Jesus for a "2nd chance" to be saved. Obviously, only God knows the "hearts" of those who repent and invite Him to be their Lord and Savior as to whether they are sincere or not. The world can only look at what we do and say. Only God can look at WHY when it comes to what we do and say.

There have been so many books, articles and movies about the rapture that it will be a "no-brainer" to understand what the rapture truly was when it occurred. Of course, the world will NEVER admit that, no matter what the circumstances are. Who wants to admit God did not want "us!" Many will try to say it was UFO's who took all these people off the planet or something else equally as ridiculous.

UFO'S FOLLOWING THE RAPTURE?

Speaking of UFO's, amazingly, the Bible tells us in Genesis 6 that for whatever reason God "allowed" some of the fallen angels to materialize and actually have sexual relations with women.

They produced offspring known as the Nephilim, meaning "giants", which were a polluted demon-human hybrid and there were enough of them over a period of time to "further pollute" the already sinful human blood line.

Some research shows they were here for at least 1000 years and this is where many of the god myths came from such as Zeus and many of the Greek gods' myths.

This is when God chose Noah and his family to build an ark that would save them from His world-wide flood. The Bible says Noah and his family were pure and this is talking about their "human bloodline" and not their holiness. This would likely explain "why" God would want to wipe out the polluted bloodline of humans and fallen angels and start over.

The Bible says about the end times in Matt 24: 27:

"That as it was in the days of Noah, so shall also the coming of the Son of man be. For as in the days that were before the flood they were eating and drinking, marrying and giving in marriage until the day that Noah entered into the ark and knew not until the flood came and took them all away. So shall the coming of the Son of man be."

This is mainly talking about how the people in Noah's day had no clue the end was about to come upon them and that it shall also be the same when Jesus comes back. The world again will have no clue what is about to befall them and that certainly applies to the world today.

Many are also saying that it is possible, and this is pure "speculation," of course, that UFO visitors might make themselves known during this time following the rapture. There are some interesting supernatural things that do occur during the 7-year tribulation period according to the book of Revelation but UFO activity and aliens/demons revealing themselves to us is not described in the book of Revelation. It is only worth mentioning due to the very large number of ever-increasing UFO activity we've been seeing the past few decades.

WHAT HAPPENS IN THE WORLD FOLLOWING THE RAPTURE?

What else does the Bible say will occur around this time? The globalists elites have been trying for many decades to bring about a one-world government. Everything we are seeing happening today is heading in that direction. The irony is they "will get" a one-world government but it is God who brings it about, not them, as this is part of God's end time plan. They will get it but they are not going to like it.

Following the rapture, the whole world will be in chaos and speculating, this may seem like a convenient time to start thinking about "we all need to live in peace and the best way to do that is to all come together and be united under a one world government".

The Bible tells us there will be a world leader that comes forward to bring this about and we know that leader as the antichrist. As I just mentioned a moment ago, the book of Daniel in chapter 9 says that the 7-year tribulation will begin when this one-world leader brings peace to the Middle East and to Israel with a peace treaty. This type of event does seem "plausible" in light of the events I just described.

The Bible also says in Ezekiel 38 that in the end times Russia and its allies, which are Persia or Iran, Iraq, Turkey and other Arab nations as well as the German area will gather together in a mighty army to finally go and attack Israel and get rid of them once and for all.

What better time to try something like this while the United States and the whole world is in major chaos due to losing millions of people from all areas of life - political leaders, military leaders, corporate leaders, etc.

Russia then might decide the United States is in no position at that time to defend Israel. They might say, "let's move fast and wipe Israel out". This is speculation but reasonably reasonable.

Ezekiel 38 describes what happens which no one expects. God Himself defends Israel and will Supernaturally destroy 5/6ths of that invading army and the whole world will "see" that God does it and "not" Israel. Even Israel will see that God Himself stepped in to save them.

People differ in opinion on "when" the Ezekiel 38 war happens. It appears to happen after the tribulation begins because Ezekiel 38 says Israel is living in safety, supposedly from the peace treaty with the world leader, and it has "unwalled" villages. Israel has major walls at this time so it appears at some point their walls will be torn down and Ezekiel 38 says "this" is the time when Russia and its allies will attack. Some believe they will attack "between" the rapture and the beginning of the tribulation. Time will tell.

PURPOSE OF THIS BOOK

This book is meant to show you God's plan is based on what scripture says and what we are seeing based on that plan as well as some of the major events that will reveal His plan and show us how it all ends. God is doing this because He wants all of us to know His plan so that we will be drawn to Him in order to have a one-on-one personal intimate relationship with Him.

God's relationship with us is "always" one-on-one. It is NOT God's relationship with "billions" but ONLY one-on-one. There is a saying – "to the world I am no one but to <u>SOMEONE</u> I am the world"! That is so incredible it should get us all "excited".

GOD'S INTIMACY AND GOD'S INSPIRED BIBLE

Remember at the very beginning I pointed out that the theme of this book is a relationship with God. That is all that God really cares about. He is not interested in acquaintances at all. He created all of us to know Him personally and to spend eternity with Him and 100 percent of the Bible is to show us God's plan from the beginning to the end and how we can have that personal relationship with Him now and forever.

It is a book of "redemption" of how mankind sinned and fell from God and what only God can do and has done to save us from our sins.

He has done it this way because He knows since He is invisible that He has to communicate with us in a way that we can understand and a way that all generations can know and understand and what better way than to have God write a "book" that explains everything.

The whole Bible was written in around 1600 years by approximately 40 different authors and fits together like a beautiful puzzle and looks like it was written by only ONE person. It was. God "inspired" those authors to write down what He wanted them to write and, of course, only He can do such a thing.

Jesus says in Matthew 24:35 "Heaven and earth will pass away but my "words" will never pass away," which reminds me - God does make a new heavens and earth at the end of Jesus' 1000-year millennial reign. More on that later.

THE WORLD REJECTS THE RAPTURE

The rapture, as I've described, will truly be one of God's "greatest" miracles when many millions of people are instantly snatched off the earth.

The world thinks we are nuts to believe anything so ridiculous. The Bible tells us that the things of God are foolishness to the world and why is that? Again, the world does not have the Holy Spirit in them to understand the "things" of God such as eternity, heaven and hell, the Bible being the Supernatural living Word of God, the rapture and many other things.

So, let's talk about the purpose of the rapture and what it is all about. You've seen where I've mentioned how the Bible tells us that born again Christians are called the "bride" of Christ. WHAT??? WHY??? You've seen where I've said several times that God wants every human being to have a personal intimate relationship with Him through Jesus and become a part of His bride. Why a bride?

GOD'S INTIMACY WITH THE HUMAN RACE

Now let's deal with the "intimate" part of our relationship with God Jesus. It is easy to understand a "personal" relationship but what do you mean by "intimate" personal relationship? The angels also have a "personal" relationship with God but not an "intimate" personal relationship.

At the beginning of this book, I mentioned how God Himself "is" a Relationship being a Triune God of Father, Son and Holy Spirit. He is actually a "3" become 1 in His own personal "intimate" Divine Relationship.

God created human beings to be able to procreate to populate and increase the human race. His way of doing this is through "marriage" where when a man and woman get married, that relationship is what God calls a "two become one" relationship. The obvious picture of two become one in marriage is sexually but it means "far more" than that.

It is a two become one relationship in doing LIFE together as two become one. It is two people bonded together in closeness and intimacy that when done God's way is the closest and most "intimate" relationship God has ever created for us. This type of "intimacy" between them is closer than any other relationship they have with anyone, including their own children.

This is the "type" of relationship God loves the "most!" In fact, it "appears" to be one of the MAIN reasons God created the human race to begin with. Our two become one intimate relationship pleases God so much that God the Father desires that His Son, Jesus, also have "this type" of personal intimate relationship with the human race and this is why when we come to know Jesus as our Lord and Savior we become born again when Holy Spirit God enters into us to make us now two become one with God!!! <u>READ THAT AGAIN, PLEASE!!!</u> THE HOLY SPIRIT IN US MAKES US TWO BECOME ONE WITH GOD!!!

This means God wants His Son Jesus to have a "bride" and get "married" to us, the human race. But just like us humans, we men will only propose to any potential bride we fall in love with who "loves us, too"! In 2 Peter 3:9 it says that God does not wish that ANY should perish but that all should come to Him through repentance.

This means the whole human race is marriage "material" to be the bride of Jesus. God, being a God of love, loves everyone but only wants to be "married" to those who love Him back. And those who "do" love Him back are those who fall in love with Jesus for who He is and what He has done to pay the price for our sins and we "desire" and actually are "amazed" that it is even "possible" to have a personal intimate relationship with God Jesus.

We repent and invite Him to be our Lord and Savior and we instantly receive Holy Spirit God in us and become a born again bride of Jesus with all of our sins paid for - past, present and future.

Can you even "begin" to fathom what God has done for us? He is allowing us to "connect" and become a part of Himself! Not angels but us filthy sinful human beings.

In Hosea 2:16 God says, "In that day, declares the Lord, you will call Me, <u>MY HUSBAND</u>. You will no longer call me Master. In verse 19 God says "I will betroth you to Me forever. You shall be <u>MY WIFE FOREVER</u>".

<u>WHY US?</u>

When I contemplate "why" God has done such a thing, I can only come up with one possible answer: We know God loves relationships. How "hard" do you think it is for one of His holy, perfect and sinless created angels to know Him, love Him and "enjoy" all that He does for them in heaven? They, obviously, don't need to have faith by being in His presence.

When it comes to marriage we often hear the phrase "opposites attract". Well, angels are not opposite to God. They are too much like God in terms of holiness but we filthy sinful lost human beings are the exact "opposite" of God in every way and thus God is attracted to us as marriage material.

God knows it's no big deal for His angels to know Him and love Him - the ones who did not fall, obviously. But God also knows that it is a "huge" deal for spiritually dead human beings to know Him and fall in love with Him since He is invisible to us and we have a sin nature.

We do not live in His presence and we have to fend for ourselves our whole lives in a sinful world vs God providing everything for us when we live in His presence.

We live our whole lives in sin without God's presence. It brings Him great "JOY" when one of us comes to know Him through faith that comes from seeing His creation and understanding that

His Word of God Bible is His instructions for saving us through Jesus which allows us to have that personal intimate relationship He so much desires for us to have with Him now and forever.

ANGELS REJOICE

This is the "biggest deal" there is when one of us through faith becomes born again. It is so huge that the Bible tells us angels "rejoice" whenever there is a new born again bride entering His kingdom.

Luke 15:10 says "In the same way, I tell you, there is rejoicing in the presence of the angels of God over one sinner who repents".

The biggest question today about the rapture is "when" is it. When will it occur? That's important but a more "important" question is "what" is the rapture? Why is it necessary?

WHAT THE RAPTURE IS FULLY EXPLAINED

Knowing that there "is" a rapture is one thing but knowing WHY makes it a LOT more UNDERSTANDABLE.

It begins with the church being the bride of Christ. As we all know, whenever a bridegroom wants to find a bride, he falls in love with someone and then he "proposes" and she either accepts his proposal or rejects it.

Since the church is the bride of Christ, did Jesus ever propose to us? The answer is YES, He absolutely did.

Jesus is a Galilean and all of His disciples are also Galileans. Most of the New Testament was written in the Galilean area and Galileans have their own customs for how they live their lives and one of their most cherished customs is their wedding customs and the steps they follow from proposing to a potential bride all the way up to the wedding ceremony itself.

At the last supper is when Jesus "proposed" to His bride the church. The Galilean custom for proposing was the bridegroom would offer his potential bride a cup of wine and if she accepted it, that meant she accepted his proposal and if she pushed the cup back, that meant she rejected his proposal.

Jesus offered His disciples a cup of wine at the last supper and they drank from it, meaning they accepted His proposal. As is the Galilean custom, Jesus then said, "I shall no longer drink from this fruit of the vine until that day when I drink it again with you in my Father's kingdom".

Also, as is part of the Galilean custom, He lets them know He will go back to His Father's house to prepare a place for them to live. When this occurs, the bridegroom leaves his bride and goes to prepare a place for them to live. In John

14:3 Jesus says:

"And if I go and prepare a place for you, I will come back and take you to be with me that you also may be where I am".

The wedding custom is the bride is now waiting for her bridegroom to prepare a place for her which often could take as long as a year or so and she is to always be pure and watch for her bridegroom to come and get her. With the church bride, the wait is only two days - God's days of 1000 years each.

One of the things very "different" about a Galilean wedding custom compared to all other Arab and even Jewish wedding customs is the Galilean custom was the "only" custom where neither the bridegroom nor the bride knew the "date" of the wedding.

The only person who knew that was the father of the bridegroom and only when he said, "son, go get your bride" would the bridegroom then leave to get his bride.

In Matthew 24:36 Jesus tells His disciples:

"But about that day or hour no one knows, not even the angels in heaven nor the Son but only the Father.

This is following the Galilean wedding customs to the T. All other cultures would assign a date for the wedding.

We, the church bride of Christ, are still in the waiting period for our Bridegroom Jesus to come and get us and take us back to heaven where He has prepared a place for us to be with Him.

When Father God tells Jesus it is time to go get Your bride, Son, "then" is when He comes to get us and that event is called the rapture when Jesus comes in the "air" for His bride.

This is described in 1 Thessalonians 4:13-18: This is Paul writing to the Thessalonian church.

"Brothers and sisters, we do not want you to be uninformed about those who sleep in death so that you do not grieve like the rest of mankind who have no hope. For we believe that Jesus died and rose again and so we believe that God will bring with Jesus those who have fallen asleep (died) in Him.

According to the Lord's Word, we tell you that we who are still alive, who are left until the coming of the Lord, will certainly not precede those who have fallen asleep

(died).

For the Lord Himself will come down from heaven with a loud command, with the voice of the archangel and with the trumpet call of God and the dead in Christ will rise first. After that, we who are still alive and are left will be caught up together with them in the clouds to meet the Lord in the air. And so, we will be with the Lord forever. Therefore encourage one another with these words.

Notice that Jesus does not come back to "earth" at that time. This is "not" His 2nd coming. He is only coming for His bride the church and He comes for us in the AIR only.

Another popular rapture verse is 1 Corinthian 15:51 that says:

"Listen, I tell you a mystery: We will not all sleep (die) but we will all be changed in a flash, in the twinkling of an eye at the last trumpet. For the trumpet will sound, the dead will be raised imperishable and we will be changed. For the perishable must clothe itself with the imperishable and the mortal with immortality.

When the perishable has been clothed with the imperishable and the mortal with immortality, then the saying that is written will come true: Death has been swallowed up in victory. Where, O death, is your victory? Where, O death, is your sting? The sting of death is sin and the power of sin is the law. But thanks be to God! He gives us victory through our Lord Jesus Christ."

These rapture verses describe perfectly the rapture event and what occurs. The next thing that happens once the bridegroom goes to get his bride is she is ready and waiting for him and she sits on a chair called a "lift" that is mounted on two poles and she is lifted into the AIR to be taken to her new home.

This is referred to as "flying the bride" to her new home. What a beautiful "picture" of the rapture where Jesus meets us in the air and we are "flown" to our new heavenly home to begin a 7-day/year wedding feast.

This is all described beautifully in a recent movie entitled "Before the Wrath". The wrath is referring to God's wrath poured out on the earth during the 7-year tribulation period. I HIGHLY recommend this movie to get "all" of the details. You can get it on YouTube and other places.

As the bride of Christ, God wants us to be alert and watching for His return. God says we are children of the day and not the night and that Jesus' coming will be like a thief in the night to an unaware world. The parable of the 10 virgins

113

talks about them having oil in their lamps in order to go out into the night to meet their bridegroom.

A very popular Christian song showing this is Midnight Cry. But God gives us enough information in His word to know the general timeframe as I have already spoken about.

The Galilean wedding custom also is when the bride and bridegroom arrive at their home, they and their guests enter through the door and the door is shut and no one can enter or leave for their wedding celebration and feast which lasts 7 days.

In our case, this 7 days is actually 7 years that lines up with the 7-year tribulation when God's wrath is poured out on the earth. There are several examples in scripture where 7 days is equivalent to 7 years and this is one of them. We, the bride of Christ, are celebrating our wedding with Him for 7 years while earth undergoes 7 years of God's wrath. The tribulation is also Daniel's 70th week which is a week of years.

Understanding the Galilean wedding customs helps us to understand not only what the rapture is about but also shows in a powerful way WHY the rapture is PRE-TRIBULATION.

GOD'S WRATH HAS A SAFE PLACE FOR HIS BRIDE

Some people who do not believe in a pre-tribulation rapture believe that the rapture happens in the middle of the tribulation or perhaps at the end of it.

Here is what they don't understand. God "always" puts His righteous in a "safe place" "before" He brings down His wrath. There are not all that many places in the Bible where we actually see God's wrath poured out on mankind. We know the earth is and has been filled with man's wrath poured out on mankind such as wars and other atrocities ever since the very beginning.

Let me give you 4 examples of God pouring out His wrath. First, in 1 Thessalonians 5:9 it says:

"For God did not appoint us (the church) to suffer "wrath" but to receive salvation through our Lord Jesus Christ".

The reason the church does not suffer God's wrath is because Jesus took on Himself God's wrath in our behalf at the cross.

In the first example, in Genesis 6, God is talking to Noah and He wants Noah and his family to enter the ark because in 7 days He is going to pour out His wrath on earth with the flood and so He is "first" putting His righteous, Noah and his family, in a "safe place," the ark, for a period of 7 (days) "before" He pours out His wrath.

In the 2nd example God sends an angel to Lot and tells Lot that he and his family are to leave Sodom and Gomorrah because God is getting ready to destroy it for its sins. This is a second example where God is taking His righteous, Lot and his family, and putting them in a "safe place" outside of the city so that God can destroy it. The angel says God will not destroy the city until Lot and his family are out of it.

In the 3rd example God is pouring out His wrath in the form of ten plagues on Pharaoh and for the 10th plague He tells Moses to put lamb's blood on the doors of God's righteous (the Jewish people) because God is coming to destroy the firstborn in Egypt. God has put His Jewish people in a "safe place" behind lambs' blood-stained doors when He pours out His wrath on Pharaoh.

The 4th example is the BIG ONE! The first three examples involved only two families and the Jewish people in Egypt. They were the righteous of God in those three examples.

In this 4th example, the "church" is the righteous of God and the church is located all over the planet. God is getting ready to bring some very serious wrath to all of the earth to punish the people for their sins but He needs to put His righteous church in a "safe place before" He pours out His wrath.

Where is the only "safe" place God can put His bride who is located all over the planet? Hopefully, this is a rhetorical question again - in HEAVEN. The rapture puts us in God's safe place so that He can pour out His wrath on the world. He even tells us about it in His Word in the "Old" Testament.

In Isaiah 26:19-21 God says:

"But your dead will live, Lord; their bodies will rise. Let those who dwell in the dust wake up and shout for joy. Your dew is like the dew of the morning. The earth will give "birth" to her dead. Verse 20 says: Go, my people, enter your rooms and shut the doors behind you. Hide yourselves for a little while until His "wrath" has passed by. See, the Lord is coming out of His dwelling to punish the people of the earth for their sins".

These verses not only describe the rapture beautifully but also tell us point blank that we will be in heaven "before" Jesus comes out to punish the people of the earth for their sins during the 7-year tribulation period.

MORE ON WHEN THE RAPTURE OCCURS

All of this shows that the rapture occurs "before" the tribulation begins and shows those who think the rapture occurs in the middle of the tribulation or at the end are simply "wrong".

If it occurred at the end of the tribulation, we saints would have to get our wedding feast "to go" because Jesus comes back with us at the very end of the tribulation following our wedding feast in Revelation 19 to set up His 1000-year millennial kingdom.

What these people are either missing or don't understand - probably the latter - is the rapture of Jesus coming for His bride in order to begin a 7 day/year wedding celebration and feast. They are totally ignoring the wedding celebration and feast.

As to when is the rapture likely to occur, I have already talked about that when I quoted Matthew 24. It is so important, let me describe it again.

Jesus narrows down the time frame quite a bit when He says that the "generation" that sees the fig tree (Israel) come back to life would be the generation that would see all these things (the end time signs Jesus describes)

That generation would see His coming (2nd coming) and the end of the age - human government age. Psalm 90:10 again defines a generation as either 70 years or 80 years with strength. Israel came back to life in 1948 and nothing happened 70 years later in 2018, so we are now looking at the 80-year generation.

The 80th year on the Hebrew calendar begins in the fall of 2028 and ends in the fall of 2029. Adding in the 0 year between BC and AD could extend it to 2030. When we subtract out the 7-year tribulation we get the fall of 2021-2023 to possibly begin the tribulation with the rapture preceding it.

None of the previous predictions for the rapture for the past few decades was right but "none" of them lined up mathematically like these years do.

COULD THE RAPTURE OCCUR THIS YEAR?

Only God knows for sure. As far as we know, everything is lined up the best we've ever seen and there are some very sharp rapture watchers on YouTube and especially on an internet show called Prophecywatchers.com who focuses on end time prophecy. If it does happen this year - YOO-HOO. There's nothing better than that for us born again believers.

If it does not occur this year, that simply means we are still in this narrow time frame of 2021 to 2023 and we continue watching and praying for Jesus to get us as soon as possible.

Today is Aug 19, 2022 and I am still writing my book and saying it is possible the rapture could occur sometime this year to 2023 as a high possible "expectation" time.

But here is the most "important" part: If the rapture does not occur in this time range, that does not change "one thing" about "everything" I have said in this book in terms of our relationship with God and the end times other than our 2021-2023 expectation years for the rapture did not occur yet. It will still be super close and we will keep watching.

If there is no rapture in this time frame there will no doubt be many who will say he is just another date setter who has been wrong like all of them have been and thus everything he is saying is wrong. There is a phrase for that - throwing the baby out with the bath. They will say he is like the little boy crying wolf over and over and people quit listening but they forget one thing - the wolf finally "did" come just like the rapture will and caught them unaware.

The signs and math for 2021-2023 have never been stronger. Obviously, 2021 has come and gone but still falls inside that 80-year generation time frame. Again, Jesus said the "generation" that saw the fig leaf Israel come back to life would be the generation that would see His coming and the end of the age.

We are looking now at an 80-year generation and Jesus' statement meant it could happen any time inside that 80 years and we are looking at the last 7 years of that 80 years.

Some people will say a generation is 100 years or 120 years, which are popular numbers but Psalm 90:10 defines it as either 70 or 80 years with strength and thus, we focus on it since only that verse defines a generation. Revelation 12 also seems to narrow down our timing even more and I will mention it next when I talk about the tribulation.

THE TRIBULATION

The book of Revelation reveals the church age followed by the 7-year tribulation. Revelation is Apocalypse which means "unveiling" - to reveal what was hidden.

The book of Revelation is the only book in the whole Bible where God promises a BLESSING to all who read it or hears it. Most pastors stay away from Revelation because many people consider it too difficult and controversial to understand. That is sad because it is one of the most important books in the whole Bible since it tells us how "everything ends".

Would you want to read an exciting book and then not read the last chapter to find out what happens? Of course not. Do you think God wants us to read and know what is in the book of Revelation? I just told you He promises a blessing to "everyone" who reads it or hears it. That is how "important it is to Him" that we all read it plus we can ask the Holy Spirit to help us understand what God is saying to us.

What makes Revelation different is it is full of symbolism and many "Supernatural" events. But it does a great job of explaining the symbolism because God wants us to understand what He is saying. There is a saying when it comes to interpreting the Bible that makes sense.

When the common sense makes sense, don't look for any   other sense or you will have nonsense.

And this most definitely applies to Revelation.

I will not be teaching on the book of Revelation but only highlighting certain key events that occur in it.

The apostle John is imprisoned on the island of Patmos for his witnessing when He has a vision from Jesus Himself. John is told to write down everything in this vision concerning the church age from what was, what is and what is to come. He wrote 7 letters to the 7 churches in that area at that time and many believe these 7 churches represent ALL churches in type and even period of time chronologically throughout church history.

If that is the case, today we are representing the church of Laodicea in which Jesus says He wishes we were either hot or cold (for Him) but we are lukewarm. Jesus says that we say we are rich but we are poor. His description for the Laodicea church is not a good one but He does end the letter by saying in

Revelation 3:20 "here I am. I stand at the door and knock. If anyone hears my voice and opens the door, I will come in and eat with that person and they with Me."

He is appealing to our less than favorable generation to invite Him into our lives to have that personable intimate relationship with Him.

There is an excellent movie "Perfect Stranger" made a few years ago of a non-believing lady lawyer who receives a dinner invitation to her favorite restaurant from someone named Jesus. She thinks her husband is playing a trick on her and she goes to have dinner there and is surprised and shocked to see a stranger waiting for her who says He is Jesus. I won't reveal any more but it lines up "PERFECTLY" with Revelation 3:20. I hope you check it out. I'm pretty sure it's on YouTube, Netflix or Prime.

The church is mentioned around 27 times in the first 3 chapters of Revelation which describes the church age "on earth" and is not mentioned again until the end of the tribulation when the church is having our wedding supper with Jesus in heaven.

Chapter 4 begins with what appears to be the rapture when John says "After this (the church age) I looked and there before me was a door standing open in heaven. And the voice I had first heard speaking to me like a trumpet said "Come up here and I will show you what must take place

"after this - the church age."

And the church is not mentioned even one time during the whole tribulation period until chapter 19 when the church is having its wedding feast with Jesus. And then is when He comes back to earth with "US" and this is His 2nd coming in which ALL eyes on earth will see Him coming in the clouds followed by us saints when He comes to set up His 1000-year millennial reign on earth.

The 7-year tribulation begins in heaven when Jesus is holding a scroll with writing on both sides and it is sealed with 7 seals that no one was able to open but Jesus Himself.

This scroll represents God's judgment to be poured out on the earth. Jesus begins by opening the first of the 7 seals which contain 7 judgments to be poured out followed by 7 trumpet judgements followed by 7 bowl judgments.

This 7-year tribulation is broken into two 3 and a half year periods called the tribulation and the "great" tribulation for the second half. There are two main purposes for the 7-year tribulation.

126

One is God pouring out His wrath to punish the people of earth for their sins. God is a very patient God but He has finally had enough and is in the process of wrapping things up for Jesus to come back and take over the planet for His 1000-year millennial reign.

The second reason for the tribulation deals with the nation of Israel. In Daniel 9 God enters into a 70 week of "years" "covenant" with the nation of Israel in which at the end of this 70 weeks of years they will receive all of the blessings God has promised them from the very beginning.

God says they will be the most prominent nation on earth and will be receiving God's blessings while finally living with their long-awaited Messiah Jesus Christ. Their rejection of Jesus at His first coming and then having Him crucified delayed them receiving their Messiah for another 2000 years.

What is very important to understand is this 70 weeks of years covenant God enters into with Israel is for Israel "alone" and not the church.

70 weeks of years is 490 years and God tells Israel in Daniel 9 that they will get everything He has promised them at the end of the 70th week.

However, Daniel 9 has this 70 weeks of years divided into 7 weeks which is 49 years and then 62 weeks which is 434 years equals 483 years. Daniel 9 says at the end of this 69th week or 483 years the Messiah will be cut off, killed, and then it starts talking about the antichrist that will come 2000 years later and begin the 7-year tribulation.

Daniel 9 also says this 70 weeks of years begins when Artaxerxes enters a decree to rebuild the city of Jerusalem around 458 BC and from that time going forward 483 years you end with Jesus entering into Jerusalem in His triumphal entry the week before He was crucified. The 490 year "clock so to speak" stopped with Jesus' triumphal entry into Jerusalem leaving the 70th week of Daniel to begin at some point in the future.

Jesus begins the church age. God's plan is He is ending

Israel's 2000 year age of the LAW and is beginning Jesus' 2000 years of grace through His church.

The church never spent even one day inside the first 69 weeks of years and there is no reason to think the church will spend even one day inside the 70th week of Daniel which begins with the 7-year tribulation.

The church also "needs" to be removed "before" the 70th week of Daniel can begin since it involves Israel and not the church. God removes His church so He can now not only bring down His wrath on mankind but also turn back to Israel and finish up Daniel's 70th week prophecy in which the Jewish people finally DO recognize Jesus as their Messiah.

They call on Him to save them at the very end of the tribulation when all the nations are gathered against them to destroy them once and for all at the battle of Armageddon.

This is when Jesus comes back with His bride - now wife - to save the Jewish people and to begin His 1000- year millennial reign as King of the earth.

Now that we know the two main reasons for the 7-year tribulation period, let's look at a few key events that occur during this period. As I said earlier, there are lots of "Supernatural" events that occur during these seven years.

Let's look at a few of them such as the antichrist is killed and supernaturally comes back to life. He has what the Bible calls a false prophet who serves him by deceiving the people into following the antichrist. He performs miracles such as calling down fire from heaven.

Also, during the first three and one half years of the tribulation Revelation tells us there will be two witnesses who will come to earth to prophesy for 1260 days clothed in sackcloth.

It does not identify them by name but from their description they appear to be Moses and Elijah. They will be able to turn water into blood which Moses did and can call fire down to destroy their enemies which Elijah did in his time.

Interesting, both of them appeared with Jesus at the Mount of Transfiguration when Jesus transfigured Himself to reveal His glory to Peter, James and John. Jesus talked with them but the Bible does not say what they talked about. It might have been something like - not yet guys but soon. That is my speculation in case you were not sure. ☺

They are protected by God during their three and a half years on earth and then God allows them to be killed at the end of the three and a half years and the whole world rejoices when that occurs and they celebrate.

Their bodies lay in the streets of Jerusalem for three and a half days and then they are resurrected and ascend back to heaven in full view of the whole world through satellites and modern technology.

God "seals" 144,000 Jewish men from the 12 tribes of Israel to witness to the world about Jesus and God Supernaturally does not allow them to be killed during this time. Angels also appear during this 7-year time period to witness.

REVELATION 12

As I mentioned earlier, the book of Revelation is full of literal and symbolic language. Chapter 12 in Revelation is referred to as the great sign in the sun, moon and stars. And it truly is a GREAT sign - far greater than most realize.

Genesis 1 tells us that God often uses signs in the sun, moon and stars to speak to us and reveal important events in scripture and Revelation 12 is certainly at the top of the list. Revelation 12 has a "lot" of symbolic language that scripture clearly reveals the answer but some of the answers are also found in other parts of the Bible.

Revelation 12 is very controversial for many people because it reveals in the sun, moon and stars a pregnant mother, a birth of a child, Satan the dragon waiting for the birth so that he can devour the child but the child is snatched up to heaven before the dragon can devour him.

WHAT??? What is that all about? The main controversy is who is the child that is born in the sun, moon and stars? But WAIT - what do you mean born in the sun, moon and stars? How is that possible?

It has to do with the alignment of the sun, moon and stars in certain astronomical alignments. The amazing thing about the universe is that planets and the sun and moon are constantly moving into different positions or alignments.

Constellations such as Virgo or Leo and the others move around into certain positions which involve the stars and the planets. God is so precise on how accurate constellation alignment is throughout the universe that we can know to the exact DAY when certain things will occur any time in the future or when they occurred any time in the past.

John in Revelation from chapter 4 on is writing about the future, the far away future and Revelation 12 is talking about the "end" close to when Jesus returns. All of this was meant for our day because we now have the technology to see these alignments in the sun, moon and stars unlike they had in the past.

I will summarize Revelation 12 here but I published a much more detailed article on the controversy in Revelation 12 in RaptureReady.com. For any of you who would like to read that article, you can click the link below. If this link does not work for some reason, Google David Cogburn Revelation 12 and you will see it there.

Before I talk about this "birth" in the sun, moon and stars I need to explain "why" there is this birth in the sun, moon and stars and what I am about to reveal is something that hardly anyone else is talking about and it will be controversial but it will explain itself in a way that makes sense.

As earlier mentioned, Mary, a virgin, was conceived by the Holy Spirit so that Jesus would not be born from the seed of man and thus, have a sin nature since that is where our sin nature comes from. Jesus' biological Father is God the Holy Spirit. When you have a "conception" you "always" have a "birth" - obviously.

Jesus is the Head of the church. Again, the Head of the church was conceived by the Holy Spirit and was born. The church is called the Body of Christ. The Body of Christ church was also "conceived" by the Holy Spirit at Pentecost. Most people will say the church was "born" at Pentecost. Born seems like the right answer "until Revelation 12". So how can we know which is accurate?

The main way again is that every "conception" is followed by a "birth". Mary was conceived by the Holy Spirit and gave birth to Jesus. If the church was "conceived" by the Holy Spirit, was it, too, "born?" The answer is "YES". The bible shows us in Revelation 12 that the church was born on September 23, 2017 in the sun, moon and stars.

That is the exact date of the male child "birth" in the sun, moon and stars in Revelation 12 and I am about to tell you where you can see the evidence for that. Since the main controversy is over who is the child that was born that day, let me quote those verses from Revelation 12.

Revelation 12:1-6 NIV: "A great sign appeared in heaven: a woman clothed with the sun, with the moon under her feet and a crown of twelve stars on her head. She was pregnant and cried out in pain as she was about to give birth. Then another sign appeared in heaven: an enormous red dragon with seven heads and ten horns and seven crowns on its heads. Its tail swept a third of the stars out of the sky and flung them to earth. The dragon stood in front of the woman who was about to give birth so that it might devour her child the MOMENT he was born. She gave birth to a male child who will rule all the nations with an iron scepter. And her child was snatched up to God and to His throne. The woman fled into the wilderness to a place prepared for her by God where she might be taken care of for 1260 days".

Do you "see" the controversy? Is the child Jesus or is it the church? She gives birth to a male child who will rule the nations with an iron scepter. That is CLEARLY Jesus and that is where those who say this child is "only" Jesus are hanging their hat. That is their evidence.

So now let's look at what they are "not" looking at in terms of "evidence". First, John is writing "only" about the future in chapters 4 through 19. If this is only Jesus, you are looking at the "past" 2000 years ago and not the future.

Second, and this is a BIGGIE - Jesus was "never snatched up" to heaven to avoid being devoured by the dragon Satan - not even close to being snatched up. Jesus "ascended" to heaven so that the Holy Spirit could come and dwell in all born again believers but certainly not to escape the dragon after His resurrection.

Herod did try to have Jesus killed, of course, but He and his family escaped to Egypt to be safe and not God's throne room. Also, the word for snatched up in Revelation 12 is "harpazo" which is the same word for the rapture of the church in 1st Thessalonians 4:13-18.

ONLY the "body of Christ church" is snatched up to God's throne room to escape being persecuted by the antichrist who is empowered by Satan and also to avoid God's wrath poured out on earth for its sins.

If you would like to check out this alignment in the sun, moon and stars on Sep 23, 2017 go to YouTube and do a search on Revelation 12 sign in the sun, moon and stars and you will see many, many videos concerning this.

This was a hot, hot topic on YouTube for the whole year of 2017 in Christian circles for those who are actually watching for Jesus' soon return. At least it was hot "until" Sep 23, 2017 when the great sign of the birth occurred in the sun, moon and stars. YouTube videos will show you "why" that is the astronomical great sign on that date.

Many of us, including myself, were thinking the rapture might be around that time because of "these" words in Revelation 12 - "the dragon stood in front of the woman who was about to give birth so that it might devour her child the MOMENT He was born". We humans know that a moment is a very quick amount of time which is fairly close to instantaneous and so there was tremendous disappointment when the rapture did not occur then.

What was being overlooked?   First, God was calling this event a "great sign".   What is a sign? A sign is something that is pointing to something "getting ready" to occur in the future.

When we are driving and we see a curve sign on the highway, we know that just ahead will be a curve we can expect.   When we see flowers and leaves coming out on plants and trees in the spring we can know that summer is near, etc.

This BIRTH on Sep 23, 2017 is a great "sign" that God is giving us WHY? Because it's time to "start watching" for Jesus to come for His bride, the body of Christ church.

This great sign and birth is actually referring to "BOTH JESUS AND HIS BODY OF CHRIST CHURCH". Jesus rules with a rod of iron and now that we are "connected" to Him through the Holy Spirit, that means that we, too, are ruling with a rod of iron.

Scripture verifies this. In Revelation 3 when John is writing to the church in Thyatira in verse 26 he says:

"To the one who is victorious and does my will to the end, I will give authority over the nations that one will rule them with an iron scepter and will dash them to pieces like pottery".

Jesus is giving the church authority to rule with a rod of iron.

The woman is Israel in Revelation 12 because only Israel flees to a place of safety from the antichrist for a period of 1260 days. Mary, obviously, never did that.

The rapture is actually the Head of the church Jesus being united with His body of Christ church when Jesus comes for His bride to take us back to heaven for our 7-year wedding celebration.

SO, what has God done here? It is HUGE! Have you noticed how God does a "lot" of HUGE things? ☺

As we know, Jesus tells us that the generation that sees the fig tree Israel come back to life will be the generation that will see His 2nd coming return to earth to rule and reign for 1000 years. And we know a generation can be 80 years.

Is there any way to "tighten up" that 80-year time period a bit? That is exactly what God has done for us. He is showing us that His great sign in the sun, moon and stars is a picture and sign of the "soon coming rapture".

God is saying "NOW" is the time you need to "start watching" because your redemption draweth near. Today we are living in God's "MOMENT" following the church's birth and being snatched up to God's throne room in the rapture.

But how long is God's moment? I mean this Sep 23, 2022 will be 5 YEARS from the birth on Sep 23, 2017. That is one long moment for sure. We also know "time" with God is vastly different than with us humans.

As I pointed out previously, in Psalms 90 and 2 Peter 3:8 it says a day with God is as 1000 years vs our 24-hour day. Revelation also describes the 7-year tribulation period as an "hour" of trial to come upon the whole earth.

Let's hope that a "moment" with God is less than the one "hour" of trial during the 7-year tribulation period. So many things are lining up "right now" to show that the rapture could, indeed, be just around the corner.

Let's now switch gears and get back to one of the most important things to occur in the 7-year tribulation that we need to watch for.

IMPORTANT, IMPORTANT, IMPORTANT - URGENT!!!

What I am about to reveal now is again one of the most important events that everyone on earth needs to know about. This is CRITICAL! In the middle of the 7-year tribulation period, the antichrist reaches a point in which he wants everyone to worship him and to "prove" you worship and support him, he forces everyone to take his "mark" on their forehead or hand with his number 666 and you must have this mark or you will not be allowed to buy or sell "anything".

And here is the most "important" part. The Bible makes it "crystal clear" that "if anyone" takes that mark, they will end up in hell forever. No exceptions.

Let me quote the verses:

Revelation 14:9-11. "A third angel followed them and said in a loud voice: If anyone worships the beast (antichrist) and its image and receives its mark on their forehead or on their hand, they, too, will drink the wine of God's fury which has been poured full strength into the cup of His wrath. They will be tormented with burning sulfur in the presence of the holy angels and of the Lamb. And the smoke of their torment will rise forever and ever. There will be no rest day or night for those who worship the beast and its image or for ANYONE WHO RECEIVES THE MARK OF HIS HAME!"

I am pretty sure there will be lots of people who are claiming to follow Jesus at that time who will do the unthinkable when it comes to taking this mark. They might pray to Jesus that they love

Him very much and they reject this antichrist person but they have a family and they have to be able to buy and sell in order to provide for their family and so they will take the mark and ask God for His forgiveness and repent for doing so. Big mistake!

The only unforgivable sin is rejecting Jesus and anyone taking the antichrist's mark is showing an outward PUBLIC "sign" of their rejection of Jesus in favor of the antichrist and since God says anyone who takes the mark is lost forever, that simply means He knows those who take the mark will have taken a "mark" that rejects Him forever.

<u>DON'T DO IT</u>! Pray big time for God's guidance and protection since you have to get through life from then on without being able to buy or sell.

Actually, we are experiencing a "preview" of this right now. Because of Covid we are seeing governments making mandates that if you don't take the Covid vaccination you won't be able to travel, fly or have a passport and many other losses of our precious freedoms.

Some places have been talking about not being able to buy and sell "already". The fact is the "technology" to even do this is already here. All of this proves that the mark of the beast technology and that governments are willing to use that technology to take away our freedoms, including the ability to buy and sell, is already being demonstrated. This is one "very important sign" to how close we are to the tribulation beginning.

WHAT HAPPENS TO THOSE WHO DON'T TAKE THE MARK?

My "assumption" is there will be millions that will not take the mark and will band together as much as possible to help one another in an "underground" type situation to get provisions that God will provide.

Also during this time, the antichrist will start persecuting Christians and Jews and many millions will be killed but the good news is the new believers will immediately end up in heaven and will come back with Jesus at His second coming and go through His 1000 year reign as a Supernatural saint vs a human being.

HOW MANY GO INTO JESUS' 1000 YEAR MILLENNIAL REIGN?

The 7 seal, trumpet and bowl judgments are devastating to the people of earth and I will not go into detail on them since this is not the purpose for this book but as I said earlier, the Bible does say that around one half of the population of earth will be killed during this time.

Here is an interesting observation. The population of earth right now is a little over 7 billion people. There could be as many as one billion that will be raptured leaving around six billion people. One half of them dying leaves three billion people. Revelation reveals that when Jesus comes back "only" those people who are His "true" believers will be allowed to enter His 1000-year millennial kingdom.

How many of the three billion left alive do you think belong to Jesus? A popular percentage of people today who are considered born again is around 25 percent. That might be a little high but twenty five percent of three billion is 750 million people remaining on earth who would enter into Jesus' 1000-year reign. Seven billion people reduced to 750 million in a 7-year period of time is almost too horrible to even imagine but we know it will occur because God's Word is never wrong.

When Jesus comes back, He will come back with His church wife and that could easily be over one billion when you consider the number raptured plus all the believers who have died for the last 2000 years and so we would actually have more Supernatural "saints" on earth than humans.

We saints will rule with Jesus and humans "visibly" and it will be the most interesting incredible time mankind has ever faced since God created us when Jesus is now running our planet.

HOW THE TRIBULATION ENDS

As we know, the tribulation is 7 years. Revelation describes it several ways - two periods of 1260 days, two 3.5 year periods, a time, time and half a time period.

There is "no question" the tribulation will end at the end of 7 years and this makes it super easy to know "around the time" of Jesus' 2nd coming. For those who study the Bible they will see that the tribulation "begins" with the antichrist signing a 7-year peace treaty with Israel and thus 7 years later would be when Jesus will be coming back.

I briefly mentioned this earlier, but the tribulation ends when Jesus comes back after 7 years to "save Israel" at the battle of Armageddon when all of the antichrist's nations are gathered against them to wipe them out once and for all. This is explained in Zechariah chapter 14.

Israel's blindness to Jesus is finally removed and they call on Him to save them and that is exactly what happens. Jesus comes back with us to Jerusalem and defeats the antichrist and his armies. He sets foot on the Mount of Olives and it immediately splits in two from east to west as shown in Zech 14 which I highly recommend you read.

Revelation does not stop with Jesus' 2nd coming. Chapter 20 tells us six times that Jesus will rule for 1000 years during His millennial reign.

JESUS' MILLENNIAL REIGN OF 1000 YEARS

Jesus is now on earth and it is time for Him to take over the planet and we enter into a 1000-year Theocracy with Jesus as our King. So, what happens during this 1000-year period with Jesus reigning? Let's get into that.

One of the major benefits of the internet is how "easy" it is to find information. You can Google Jesus' 1000-year millennial reign and see many well written articles that go into far greater detail on what happens and what this time period will be like. I will give you a few highlights of what occurs.

Jesus' 1000-year millennial reign is a "major" part of God's plan for mankind. It will be unlike any other time in human history. Why? Because God Jesus has come back to earth to be visible to mankind and to govern our planet.

God left the planet when Adam and Eve sinned. When He came back in the form of a human Jesus Christ, His mission then was to save us from our sins on the cross and the "world" did not recognize Him as Supernatural God at that time.

When He comes back the 2nd time, He comes to "judge" the world and He comes back in the clouds and all eyes will see Him and He comes back as fully recognizable God to rule and reign. No mistaking Him this time. I think most people are familiar with the term lamb and lion as used in the Bible. Jesus came the first time as the Lamb to be sacrificed for our sins and He comes back the second time as the Lion to be King and rule the earth.

DIFFERENCES OF MILLENNIAL REIGN COMPARED TO NOW

The most obvious and major difference in Jesus' millennial reign compared to now is Jesus will visibly be ruling the planet and we, His new wife and saints, will be ruling alongside Him. As I said, it appears there will be more saints on earth at that time than human beings - at least until their population exceeds ours. We will be living and interacting visibly with humans in every way. More on that in a moment.

The first thing that needs to happen when He comes back and defeats the antichrist and his armies is Jesus sends out His angels to gather up His true believers and unbelievers.

Matthew 25 refers to this as Jesus separating the sheep from the goats in which all people will be brought before Jesus at His 2nd coming and ONLY the sheep or those who truly belong to Jesus will be allowed to enter into His 1000-year millennial reign and the goats will go into eternal punishment.

We also know from Scripture that during Jesus' reign there will be no more wars and the earth will be "restored" back to the way it was at the beginning when people lived to be hundreds of years old.

Isaiah 65:20 says: "Never again will there be in it an infant who lives but a few days or an old man who does not live out his years. The one who dies at a hundred will be thought a mere child and the one who fails to reach a hundred will be considered accursed. Isaiah 11:6 says "and the wolf will dwell with the lamb and the leopard will lie down with the young goat and the calf and the young lion and the fatling together. Isaiah 11:8 says a child will play safely with the cobra.

So, clearly things are very different then compared to now. Many people today consider the planet over populated and over-crowded and we need "less" people. As I mentioned earlier, it is possible there could be less than one billion humans beginning Jesus' 1000-year reign. BUT with people living to be hundreds of years old again and there being far less death than before, can you even begin to imagine how many "billions" of people there will be in "1000 years" living on earth during a time like this?

DIFFERENCE BETWEEN SAINTS AND HUMANS

I mentioned a moment ago about how we saints will be living alongside earth's human beings. We saints will be far different from humans at that time. We will be Supernatural beings able to do things humans will not be able to do.

I will talk more on that when I talk about heaven. A fun thought I like to imagine is going to the golf course with one of my human friends and asking him if I can borrow his driver to tee one up. I cannot imagine what that might be like.

Humans will probably still work for a living. We just won't know for sure how that works until that time comes. God takes care of everything inside eternity for His eternal beings. How commerce and life for all of us will be during Jesus' millennial reign is speculative in terms of will the internet still be viable and working? If so, I think we can safely assume there will no longer be any porn or bad stuff on it.

How about for us saints? Where will we live? I'm pretty sure we will not be working for money or need money. Humans also have to sleep. We will not have to sleep. In heaven there is no longer any night and sleep will no longer be necessary for us. We will be fully "energized" at all times, especially since we are connected to God.

I am now speculating with a "reasonable assumption" that we might have access to heaven and the new Jerusalem, which I will mention in a moment, any time we need to be there. A sneak preview of abilities is that teleportation appears to be one of our gifts.

Philippians 3: 20-21 says: "But our citizenship is in heaven. And we eagerly await a Savior from there, the Lord Jesus Christ, who, by power that enables Him to bring everything under His control, will transform our lowly bodies so that they will be like His glorious body.

HUMANS DURING THE MILLENNIAL REIGN

For the humans who enter into Jesus' millennial reign, it won't take long before they start having children and their children start having children and soon there will be millions and billions of people who have never known life on earth before Jesus came back. They will be "shocked" to discover what life was like on earth before Jesus in terms of wars, diseases, politics, etc.

It needs to be pointed out though that every human being, even in Jesus' millennial reign, still will have a sin nature because every human being is still born with that sin nature from their human father's seed.

SIN STILL PRESENT DURING THE MILLENNIAL REIGN

The Bible tells us that Satan will be bound during this 1000- year reign of Christ so that no one will be able to say any longer – "the devil made me do it".

You would think that every human being that is born with Jesus and His saints ruling the planet would automatically fall in love with Jesus and want to belong to Him but that is not the case.

You would think that when humans see us saints and see how holy we are and all the things we can do that they cannot do, that they, too, would be looking forward to that day when they will also be saints.

The problem is that the sin nature works differently on different people and especially in the realm of free will and many do reject Jesus and eternity with Him as you are about to see.

HUMAN CONVERSATIONS WITH SAINTS

There is one thing for sure: people will no longer be able to say God, Jesus and the Bible are not true. There will be "no" other so-called religions. Everyone will know the "truth" of the Bible and heaven and hell.

I can only imagine what types of conversations there will be between saints and humans during this time. I imagine there will be many humans who will want to know tons about heaven and what it is like. They might even ask saints to take a video camera to heaven which I am pretty sure would be forbidden as heaven is only accessible to eternal sinless beings and it appears God does not want to ruin the wonderful surprises for all who go there.

I would think many will also be asking about hell and what is that like and when they find out how real and how horrible it is, you would think no one would ever want to go there and everyone would avoid it by loving Jesus.

JESUS RULES WITH AN IRON ROD

Why would they not love and want to follow Jesus? The answer is always as I mentioned - "sin nature".

As we know Jesus rules the planet with an iron rod. Why does He need to do that? Because every human "still" has a sin nature and many will not like at all Jesus' iron rod way of ruling them when they would rather follow their sin nature in terms of living their lives.

There will be no need to rule with an iron rod "after" God makes the new heavens and new earth and we are finally done with the sinful human race.

In eternity we will be living on the new earth with God, Jesus and the Holy Spirit "forever" and with no sin anywhere, there is no need for any kind of iron rod – especially since we are now connected to God through the Holy Spirit.

SOME QUESTIONS ABOUT THE MILLENNIAL REIGN

But in the millennial reign will there be guns and murder and violence during that time? We are not sure. I would be surprised if guns and weapons like that are still around but we can't know for sure now. Violence will probably still be around due to people's sin natures getting angry and hurting other people from time to time.

Will there be crime? Possibly but I doubt if anyone could get away with stealing or other types of crimes due to Jesus and His saints controlling everything. I can't imagine someone committing a crime and all of us saints saying gee, I wonder who did that? We won't need Columbo for those old enough to know who he is. He is still on reruns though.

WHAT HAPPENS AT THE END OF THE MILLENNIAL REIGN

But what happens is the millennial reign of Jesus lasts 1000 years and at the end of that 1000 years Satan is released from the Abyss to go out to the four corners of the earth to gather his followers for battle.

In Revelation 20 it says "In number they are like the sand on the seashore. They marched across the breadth of the earth and surrounded the camp of God's people, the city he loves. But fire came down from heaven and devoured them and the devil who deceived them was thrown into the lake of burning sulfur where the beast and the false prophet had been thrown. They will be tormented day and night forever and ever".

It is unbelievably sad to think of the millions if not billions who have rejected Jesus as the millennial reign comes to a close. They will know 1000 percent that hell is real and horrible and that heaven is great and wonderful and still reject Jesus "knowing" without a doubt they will end up in hell for eternity.

Today because Jesus and God's kingdom are still invisible, people can reject Jesus with at least a "false hope" that they are correct and hell is not real.

This type of false hope will not exist during Jesus' Millennial reign when He has been ruling the planet for 1000 years. The people who reject Jesus then have ZERO excuse for doing so other than somehow in some sadistic way hell seems better to them than heaven.

Things might be different if God gave every human a one- hour taste of heaven and a one-hour taste of hell and "then" have them choose but God is not going to beg anyone to come spend eternity with Him and especially when He shows them the "truth" of eternity and how "easy" it is to belong to Him.

Satan is released for a short time "after" the 1000 years is over. He gathers his followers, fire comes down from heaven to destroy them and "then" we have the great White Throne judgment in which all unbelievers of all ages are judged.

Chapter 20 shows us that following Jesus' 1000-year millennial reign there will be the great White Throne judgment. This is an eternal judgment in which all "unbelievers" of all time will appear before the Lord to be judged based on their "works" and as we already know, "works" cannot get anyone into heaven.

All born again believers' names are written into God's book of life, also called, the Lamb's book of life and at the great White Throne judgment, anyone whose name is not written in the Lamb's book of life, which is all of them, are judged and end up in hell.

WHAT HAPPENS FOLLOWING THE GREAT WHITE THRONE JUDGMENT

Chapter 21 and 22 tell us what happens following the great White Throne judgment. At this time is when God makes a new heavens and a new earth. He does this because our present earth and universe are corrupted due to man's sin and God makes a new heavens and new earth without sin since the age of human beings is now over with.

Our present sinful universe which creates time will be over with and God then makes a new heavens and universe with no more time but only eternity. That bubble universe with time in it that I mentioned at the beginning of the book is destroyed leaving only eternity once again.

THE NEW JERUSALEM

Revelation 21 shows us that God has created a New Jerusalem city in heaven for us that is very amazing and unique. This new Jerusalem will descend from heaven down to the new earth.

What is amazing is the size of this new Jerusalem. It is right at 1500 miles long, wide and tall. There is a debate as to the shape of it but most people describe this city as a cube.

However, those dimensions also apply to a pyramid shape. I do find it interesting that there is so much mystery about the great pyramid of Giza in Egypt in terms of all of the things it represents and reveals and especially as to how it was constructed and by whom.

The Bible says there is an ALTER "to the Lord" in the heart of Egypt and this appears to be where the great pyramid of Giza is located.

Isaiah 19:19 In that day there will be an alter to the Lord in the heart of Egypt, and a monument to the Lord at its border.

Is the great pyramid of Giza a small "replica" of our eternal new Jerusalem that God put on earth from almost the very beginning? Maybe. Maybe not. It sounds like something God might do. That topic is certainly debatable.

Right now if we go up into the air like 200 or more miles we are already in space. The new Jerusalem goes up 1500 miles. All of this is described in Revelation 21 in detail. Earth and space will be obviously different at that time and space will not be dangerous to us in any way since we are no longer humans. Revelation 21 and 22 go into quite a bit of detail to describe what is going on and what things look like. I will leave that for you to read. Jesus ends the Bible in chapter 22 telling us He is coming SOON. Let's not forget that two 1000-year days is "soon" for God.

HEAVEN

Now we get into a FUN topic for sure. Heaven is a place that "most" of the human race desires to go to. Why is that? Number one is because it is an "eternal" place and shows that our tiny, tiny lifespan on earth is not over when we die but simply beginning our now new eternal life. Notice I did not say lifespan. There is no "span" connected to eternal.

Number two is because heaven is where most humans think or know is the place where God lives and God represents infinite power, love, goodness and every other good thing that is imaginable. God will take care of "everything for everybody" for all eternity.

As stated previously, even those who deny God and say they don't believe in him are simply lying to themselves as God has "instinctively" revealed Himself through the universe, all life on earth and through His holy Word of God Bible.

Number three is most humans also know about hell and no way want to go there. It is to be avoided at all costs since it is a place where God does not dwell and without God and all of His goodness, you get the opposite when you spend eternity without God. We are talking about eternal darkness, pain, torment and all things bad and unpleasurable forever.

MORE INFORMATION ON HEAVEN

Hopefully, by now you have seen how this book has shown you that God loves us more than we can imagine and desires above all things a personal, intimate relationship with each of us to join Him as part of the bride of Jesus.

The Bible talks quite a bit about heaven and there are many good books out there that go a lot more into depth about what heaven is like. Randy Alcorn wrote an excellent book on it entitled "Heaven" and I highly recommend it.

What is important when we look at heaven and examine it is that we not "guess" at how things will be there but see what God's word says about it and look through scripture for any evidence that further demonstrates life in heaven.

HEAVEN'S DIFFERENCES AND HOW OUR BODIES ARE DIFFERENT

So, where do we start? We start with Jesus, of course. Jesus is God. Jesus came to earth. Jesus tells us things about heaven and gives us some insight as to what some things will be like.

Let me repeat again how the Bible says our bodies will be like Jesus.

Philippians 3:21 Jesus says "who by the power that enables Him to bring everything under His control will transform our lowly bodies so that they will be like His glorious body".

The first thing that is different is our bodies. We all will have new resurrection bodies, which we get at the rapture, that never die or get sick or feel pain and can do many things that our human bodies cannot.

We will have "spiritual" bodies and not flesh and blood human bodies. I seriously doubt we will need bathrooms any more or even bedrooms since there is no night or any kind of "darkness" in eternity. The Bible says our light will come from God Himself.

We will not age because we are eternal and we will all know each other and never have to be introduced to anyone. Why is that? Probably because we are all "connected" to God through the Holy Spirit and we are all the bride of Jesus and will become His wife. Jesus does not have billions of wives but one wife - the Body of Christ church with Him as the Head.

A good example in the Bible of us seeming to be able to know everyone occurred at the Mount of Transfiguration in Matthew 17:1-8. Jesus was there to pray with Peter, James and John and He was transfigured from His human body into His glorified radiant body.

While there two Old Testament prophets, Moses and Elijah, appeared with Him and Jesus had a conversation with them. Peter, James and John "recognized" them as Moses and Elijah. They did not have to be introduced to them and this could be a preview of how things will be in eternity.

Following Jesus' resurrection, He came back to spend time with His disciples and was here for 40 days and had the ability to do things then that He did not do before.

He tells His disciples our new resurrected bodies will be like His. Twice when the disciples were together behind locked doors Jesus instantly appeared before them. That means that He simply teleported into their room. Since our bodies will be like His, that means we, too, will be able to teleport in heaven and all eternity. For us eternity will begin with heaven and then we move to the new heavens and new earth following Jesus' 1000-year millennial reign.

What is teleportation all about? I call it "instant travel". But somehow God gives us the ability to be "anywhere" instantly whether somewhere else in heaven or perhaps somewhere in outer space. I mentioned earlier that with teleportation we could instantly travel between heaven and earth during Jesus' 1000-year millennial reign.

Our Supernatural bodies will never die, get sick or feel pain. We will be "comfortable" wherever we are. We could teleport to the bottom of a lake or to the middle of the sun or anywhere in outer space and be "comfortable". We certainly will not have to breathe or do anything else a flesh and body has to do.

Also, we know New Jerusalem is 1500 miles long, wide and tall. Suppose we are at the top and want to go to the bottom. Do you think we will have to take an elevator up and down? Do you know how long it takes for a 747 to travel 1500 miles? But with teleportation it would be instantaneous or we might simply fly down.

When Jesus ascended back to heaven, gravity was no problem for Him. It appears we will be able to fly in heaven. A good example of this is when Jesus comes back at His 2nd coming, He comes in the AIR and we are with Him and we are not wearing parachutes. Technically we are on horses but we can also know that if horses can fly, then flying would be no problem for us saints. And let us not forget that we meet Jesus in the "AIR" at the rapture. I personally think God will bless us with flying for the sheer fun of it.

WORSHIP IN HEAVEN

One of the most important things we will "LOVE" to do in eternity is worshiping God. Unfortunately, many people look at heaven now as one long boring church service. I think this applies more to non-born again church goers than born again church goers.

I can assure you that when we are in the "presence" of Jesus, worship will be at the top of our list of things we look forward to. We will enjoy giving thanks, honor, gratitude and glory to the Lord who created us for Himself and gives us far more forever than we can ever imagine.

An interesting thought about worship is this: It appears there will be billions of people and angels in eternity and when we come together to worship the Lord, do we all come together at one time?

Can you imagine how "large" a crowd of one billion saints and angels would be, let alone billions plural. A billion saints standing next to one another would reach out dozens and dozens of miles or so if not hundreds of miles.

I have not done the math, but we have seen crowds here reported as large as one million and they stretch out quite a distance. One billion is 1000 million and I think you get the idea of how large that would be. But, that is "no biggie" - no pun intended - for God. It shall be exciting to see how that occurs in eternity.

HOW DO WE HAVE ACCESS TO JESUS?

My next observation about something "HUGE" in heaven is 100 percent speculation on my part but it makes a lot of sense to me and so I'll share it.

With billions of people loving the Father, Son and Holy Spirit and wanting to be with Jesus as much as possible, how do you think that happens? Do we call up and make an appointment and have to wait hundreds of our earth years to see Him? I am not sure but I doubt it will be like that. Why? Because we are "connected" now to God. We are Jesus' bride now and His wife in heaven.

The Holy Spirit is invisible to us now and the Holy Spirit is "everywhere". The Holy Spirit might function differently in eternity. It just might be that in eternity if we want to be with Jesus that all of us might be able to do so by Him appearing to us through the Holy Spirit. He could be with millions at the same time if it works that way. Again, this is "pure speculation" and is just an interesting thought but to me it sounds plausible.

OUR GREATEST MOMENT

If you were to ask me what is the greatest "moment" you could ever imagine happening to you now or in eternity, the answer for me is instant and nothing else comes close. Just picture in your mind you are in heaven and Jesus comes up to you and wraps His arms around you and holds you tight. We are talking about goose bump city here! But Jesus, the Creator of all things is holding YOU alone in His arms. That will be incredible, to say the least.

IS THERE WORK IN HEAVEN?

What about work? Will we work in heaven? The Bible makes it clear that there will be different degrees of responsibility for each of us in eternity. However, "work" will be far different in eternity than on earth and especially in terms of "enjoyment".

It makes sense God will bless each one of us with some sort of work that is perfectly suited for each of us and that we all will have a passion for. You know what they say about passion - that if your work is your passion, you never have to work a day in your life.

Work is about progress and God never stands still. We have no clue of all of the "incredible" things God has in store for us throughout eternity. You can rest assured it will not be an eternal vacation but much, much more rewarding than that.

NON-BIBLICAL SOURCES FOR HEAVEN

I am sure most of us are aware of what is called near death experiences. I have been following NDE's for many years as I find them fascinating. For those who may not know, a NDE is where someone physically dies for a short time and gets a glimpse of the afterlife.

One of the most amazing things is how many people have NDEs. Research it and you will see it is in the millions and as we know, many people have written books about their NDE and some of these books are best sellers.

Why is that? Because almost all of us are curious and interested in the afterlife in terms of is it real and if so, what is it like?

The first question many of us wonder when we hear or read about someone having a NDE is whether it is "real" or not. I mean just because someone says it's real, unfortunately, does not mean it is. Are they writing a book based on a lie just to make money? This may shock you but yes, some people really do it for that reason.

But there are also people who truly did have the NDE they are talking about and they "want" everyone to know what they experienced so that it might bring hope and encouragement to many who desperately want to know the truth about life after death. So, is there any way to discern who is telling the truth and who is not and yes, there is a way to narrow it down.

IS A NDE TRUE DEATH?

First, it is important to know that a NDE is not a true death because it is not "eternal" death. It appears to be an in between place God seems to allow some people to experience a glimpse of the afterlife in some way.

Most of them will describe a door or some sort of barrier they were not allowed to cross or else they would not be able to come back. That barrier is "eternity". Do not forget that what happens in eternity "stays" in eternity. Each person that had a true NDE and came back never actually entered into eternity and so let's examine things to look for when trying to discern how real a particular NDE is.

WHAT TO LOOK FOR WHEN EXAMINING THE TRUTH OF A NDE

The most important "gauge" to look at and compare to is always God's Word in the Bible. As mentioned, the Bible tells us a lot about heaven and eternity. Any true NDE will not contradict "anything" in the Word of God Bible.

Why every NDE "has" to line up with God's Word is because Satan is the great deceiver. He would "love" for the world to think that all of these NDEs "prove" everyone goes to heaven when they die and nothing could be further from the truth.

There are NDE's that talk about hell and I think the main reason we don't hear a lot more about the hell NDE's is because people who have them do not want to talk about them for obvious reasons and never make them public.

For me when I read about "any" NDE I take it with a grain of salt. If everything lines up with scripture, I certainly enjoy the thought of that person's experience more than if they say things that contradict scripture.

CHARACTERISTICS OF MANY NDE'S

Some of the common characteristics of NDE's is people die for a short time, often in a hospital setting, and they leave their body and start observing what is going on while they are unconscious or dead. Some are able to describe events that occurred in the operating room or even in other places in the hospital such as people praying for them or eating or doing other things, which is evidence their NDE was real when they come back and report on it.

And after leaving their body they travel often through a tunnel to a bright source of light and meet up with an angel or angels or family members who had died or in some cases with Jesus Himself.

It seems that most describe seeing their whole life laid out before them and see the good, bad and ugly during their lifetime. They experience a life review.

Almost all of them with good NDE's talk about the intense incredible "love and peace" they felt while there. Quite a few do talk about how "vibrant" everything is in terms of color, sound, music, etc. They say the grass and flowers are so intense in colors that words can never adequately describe them.

Many also talk about lots of flying and others talk about being able to communicate telepathically by thought. Some talk about binocular vision where they could zoom in and see things many miles away. These are just a few of the incredible things these people claim to have experienced in their NDE's.

CREDIBILITY TO LOOK FOR

The ones that seem to have the most credibility are the ones who saw things happening on earth while they were dead and described them in great detail. Others talk about meeting relatives whom they never even knew on earth such as grandparents or great grandparents and their description of what happened with them in their NDE was verified by those here who knew those people such as grandparents and great grandparents.

NDE'S VS THE BIBLE

The bottom line for me with NDE's is I find the ones that line up with scriptural accuracy the most interesting but I always put my faith in ONLY what the Bible says.

We do know in the Bible different people did experience dreams and visions. The apostle Paul claims He visited the third heaven and received information that he was not allowed to share with us. This certainly lines up with there are some things about eternity God does not want us to know YET!

Now John in Revelation was taken up to heaven in vision or some other way and saw all of the amazing things he saw and he was "commanded" to write it all down because that is something God WANTS all of us to know and will bless us when we read it or hear it.

WATCHING GOD CREATE A NEW HEAVENS AND UNIVERSE

As I mentioned earlier, following the great White Throne judgment is when God creates the new heavens and new earth. I assume we will all get to "see" Him do this. Can you imagine watching God create the new heavens and earth? WOW is all I can say.

This is when the new Jerusalem comes down from heaven onto the new earth and we then begin "eternity" with no more sinful human beings. The 7000 years of the human race is over and it will be even more wonderful to know we now live in eternity where there is "no more sin".

GOD HAS MORE PLANS FOR US IN ETERNITY THAN WE CAN IMAGINE

And as to the things God has in store for us during eternity He describes in His word.

1 Cor 2:9 "But as it is written: Eye hath not seen, nor ear heard, neither have entered into the heart of man the things which God hath prepared for them that love Him".

God is saying basically that there are many things we have "no clue" about which God has in store for us in eternity and they will be incredible beyond words. Hallelujah!

CONCLUSION

Concerning God's plan, let's ask ourselves this question: What has God "truly" done and WHY did He do it this way? Some of this will be redundant but should be said again to wrap things up.

When it comes to sentient beings that God has a relationship with, we have angels and we have humans. Angels and humans are as different as night and day. All angels were created directly by God and are holy, sinless and perfect - the two-thirds that did not fall, obviously. They dwell in heaven and eternity with God. God provides "everything" for them and they enjoy the very

BEST God has to offer at this time, as I explained before.

We humans are the exact OPPOSITE of angels. The Bible says we are created in God's image. That is super important in terms of what God does and why He does it. We do not live with God in heaven or inside eternity yet.

We are born with a sin nature that makes us anti-God from birth and we are born spiritually dead. To go from being spiritually dead to spiritually alive is something that is impossible for us to do on our own. We need help. We need to be spiritually resurrected from death to life. Salvation is about only ONE thing - NO SIN, period. It is "that simple!"

Doing good deeds and good works is nice no matter how many good things we do. You could be as good as a Mother Teresa 100 times over and you are still spiritually dead without a personal relationship with God through Jesus. This is why WORKS means "nothing" in terms of gaining entry into heaven.

Father God knows this. He knows we human beings don't have a chance of saving ourselves and only He can save us.

This is why He decided to send God Jesus to earth to perform the greatest act of love there is - to DIE, Himself, on a cross in order to save us by removing our sins and giving us His righteousness. God Jesus paid the price for our sins and when we begin a personal, intimate relationship with Him, ALL of our sins are REMOVED FOREVER and we go from being spiritually dead to spiritually alive.

When we do good deeds now, the good deeds have ZERO to do with earning salvation. But when we do them to please and serve the Lord, the Bible tells us we earn "eternal rewards". We won't fully understand how that works until we get to heaven, but, of course, it is very important.

Good works while spiritually dead means nothing eternally and good works while spiritually alive means eternal rewards. What a difference!

The biggest difference between angels and humans is no sin vs sin. Two-thirds of God's "saved" angels remained saved after one-third fell from God's grace. The opposite is what has happened to the human race. Two-thirds of God's lost humans with their sin nature remain lost while around one-third become saved through Christ.

Does this seem fair? Two-thirds of the angels remained saved and only one-third of the humans became saved. From our human perspective this does not seem fair but let's look at it from God's perspective.

What I am about to say right now and what I have already said throughout this book is not just my opinion or speculation. It is based directly on what the Bible says or on what has "happened" as revealed by God's plan in His holy Bible. I have speculated some and have mentioned it when I did.

God loves His angels, and they love Him and thus for them to "know" God is no big deal since they are already holy, sinless, perfect beings and are dwelling with Him in heaven.

God loves us humans, too, but we are behind the 8 ball ALL of our lives due to our sin nature. Without Christ the best we can hope for is whatever good pleasures we can achieve from living a life that is so short compared to eternity that it can barely be measured and then it is eternity separated from God. Not a pleasant thought!

So, compared to angels is it a BIG DEAL for us sinful humans to fall in love with invisible God through faith as evidenced by what we see in creation and what we know through His Word in the Bible while having to live our whole lives on sinful earth taking care of ourselves compared to angels?

To GOD, it's the BIGGEST DEAL there is. There is nothing bigger than when a sinful human being falls in love with God through God Jesus taking all our sins onto Himself.

This explains why only around one-third of the human race becomes born again and becomes "connected" to God through Holy Spirit God. Obviously, God is saddened that more humans don't become born again but the ones who do become born again bring God more pleasure than the sadness from those who don't.

The bottom line is the GREATEST thing God has ever done is create a sinful human race to be able to know Him through His Son Jesus and become a PART OF HIM - a two become one intimate relationship, as I explained earlier.

God wants us to join Him and become a part of Himself and He wants to do it with us filthy sinful human beings partly because we have to live our whole human lives in a sinful body in a sinful universe and what greater REWARD can there be than being connected to God forever in eternity.

In eternity we will have free will but unlike the angels who also have free will and can actually goof up and sin, that will be impossible for us because we are a part of God and just like God would never sin, we will never sin and we will be able to LOVE like God loves. To love "like God" is beyond human comprehension.

It is mind-boggling to see what God has done by creating the human race and desiring us to connect with Himself. I am not sure we are even capable of fully understanding what all that means now and certainly we will not know what it will mean in eternity until we get there but we CAN KNOW it is bigger and better than anything we can imagine now. Please let "all" of this soak in and draw you closer to the Lord. It is exciting beyond words!

And here is another wonderful thought. We now think of Triune God as Father, Son and Holy Spirit. But God has added us born again believers to Himself through the Holy Spirit to where "technically" now it is God the Father, Son, Holy Spirit and His adopted children.

Actually, in eternity we are the daughter-in-law to God the Father, the wife to God Jesus and I see Holy Spirit God as our LINK and communicator in our intimate relationship with God Jesus and Father God. That is speculation on my part and appears to be a debatable issue so we'll have to wait - and probably not very long - to see how it all unfolds.

HOW TO BECOME BORN AGAIN

I mentioned in this book at the end I would show everyone how easy it is to become a born again Christian and bride of Christ. But here is a question each one of us has to answer for ourselves and it is the most important question to every human being on the planet.

This is a long sentence, but if you knew 1000 percent beyond a shadow of a doubt that Creator God created you, loves you beyond measure, knows you more than you know yourself and desires to come into your life to have a personal, intimate relationship with you now and to help guide you on the rest of your journey through life and then be with Him forever in eternity, is that something you would truly DESIRE???

If so, all you need do is to acknowledge that you are a sinner who needs Jesus to take away your sins in order to become a born again Christian and His bride.

REPEAT THE SINNER'S PRAYER

Lord Jesus, I recognize I am a sinner and I repent of all of my sins. I can never thank you enough for dying on a cross to pay the price for my sins. I invite you to come into my life to be my Lord and Savior and to help me live a life that pleases you. In Jesus' precious name I pray, Amen.

Now it is important to know that those words alone did "not" save you. It is your "HEART" that saves you. God "knows" if you are serious and truly desire to know Him and have that saving personal, intimate relationship with Him.

I hope and pray that many of you, indeed, are desiring that with this prayer. I have a Christian slogan that says it pretty well. When it comes to salvation, the heart of the matter is a matter of the heart!

MY GOAL IN WRITING THIS BOOK

My main goal in writing this book is to show you God's plan in a way that, hopefully, has been fairly easy to understand. If you have never read the Bible or know very little about the Bible, then I pray that God opens your eyes, your mind and your heart to understand a lot more of His plan and what He is up to.

I mentioned at the beginning that if you finish this book, your understanding of God's plan will be "off the charts" compared to where you were before you read this book and I pray that is the case.

I also pray that God Jesus will open your heart to now fall in love with Him and desire Him above all things. You will be "amazed" at how, although invisible, He will change your life in a way you never thought possible and will give you a peace and contentment that the whole world can only dream of.

GETTING STARTED

The best way to get started is by first praying and talking with the Lord on a daily basis. God's children think of Him daily and often - not just on Sundays.

Think of Jesus as your best friend because He truly is. Yes, He is still invisible, but I promise He can communicate with you in a way that you will "know" He is with you every moment of your life because you now have God the Holy Spirit residing in you and connecting you to Himself.

A personal relationship with God Jesus is the same as any other important relationship in terms of what do you do when you love someone? You want to be with them, talk with them and spend time with them and you can actually do this much "easier" with Holy Spirit God than with people because Holy Spirit God is now in you every second of every day.

Obviously, it will be MUCH BETTER when we are with Jesus face to face but God is so incredible that even though He's invisible, He can relate to us in a way that we can sense Him, know Him and enjoy Him while we journey through this sinful world toward our eternal Home to be in His Presence forever.

Our love for God cannot come close to how much He loves us. Your desire to be with Him pleases Him mightily.

FIND A GOOD BIBLE CHURCH

The next step is "important". Seek God's help in finding a good Bible believing church. If you do not go to church, pray about and ask God and people you know who love the Lord to help you find a good "bible believing" church that believes the Bible is the infallible, inerrant word of God and Jesus is its main focus. You would be surprised at how many churches are not good bible believing churches.

Joining a good church is one way God can guide us and help us to grow quickly in what to do in our

188

walk with Him through the rest of our life toward eternity.

God will help us to find a new "family" of like-minded believers who fellowship together, pray together, support each other together and grow closer to the Lord together.

But start reading the Bible. Start with the book of John in the New Testament if you are not sure where to start. It focuses on Jesus being the Son of God. Remember, the Bible is God's instruction manual to us and you can only get better at "anything" when you read, study and apply the MANUAL!

Go online and ask the Lord to help you find material that will help you to start growing as a born again child of God. The Holy Spirit will guide you as you seek to grow as a new believer desiring to know more of the Bible and to please the Lord in all you do. You will start growing NOW and you continue to grow until the day you see Jesus in person.

Let me conclude by thanking you for reading my book. I pray it's been a blessing to you and don't forget that everything is pointing to Jesus coming for His bride soon - possibly weeks to months.

Only God knows the date for sure but He loves it when we are <u>waiting, watching and ready for His return</u>. He loves it so much that He gives all of us "watchers" what is called the <u>CROWN OF RIGHTEOUSNESS</u> when we are finally with Him. Many blessings to each and every one of you.

Maranatha! Come quickly, Lord Jesus.

davidcogburn80@gmail.com

Printed in Great Britain
by Amazon